PRINT AND PRODUCTION FINISHES FOR

Bags, Labels, and Point of Purchase

A RotoVision Book

Published and distributed by RotoVision SA
Route Suisse 9
CH-1295 Mies
Switzerland

RotoVision SA
Sales and Editorial Office
Sheridan House, 114 Western Road
Hove BN3 1DD, UK

Tel: +44 (0)1273 72 72 68
Fax: +44 (0)1273 72 72 69
www.rotovision.com

10 9 8 7 6 5 4 3 2 1

ISBN: 978-2-940361-94-6

Art Director: Tony Seddon
Design: Morris and Winrow
Additional photography: Simon Punter

Reprographics in Singapore by ProVision Pte.
Tel: +65 6334 7720
Fax: +65 6334 7721

Printed in Singapore by Star Standard
Industries (Pte.) Ltd.

PRINT AND PRODUCTION FINISHES FOR

Bags, Labels, and Point of Purchase

Carolyn Knight and Jessica Glaser

RotoVision

CONTENTS

Mode 002

La Mode

Buy Now
For Sale

Written, produced and
arranged by Steve Angello
& Sebastian Ingrosso.
Recorded at Oversized
Studios Stockholm for
La Mode 2005. Published
by Universal Publishing.
Manufactured by Euro Disc.
Distributed by Unique
Records and Distribution
UK. Made in Sweden.

BWO

Temple Of Love The Club Mixes

0946 358027 2 6. BIEM/ncb, bel/BIEM
Made in EU. LC 0142. ℗ 2006 EMI Music
Sweden AB. © 2006 EMI Music
Sweden AB. All rights of the producer and of the
owner of the recorded work reserved.
Unauthorized copying, hiring, renting,
public performance and broadcasting of
this record prohibited. This label copy
information is the subject of copyright
protection. All rights reserved. © 2006
EMI Music Sweden AB.

Capitol Music from EMI

INTRODUCTION

Global consumerism has secured a prominent role for the graphic design of bags, labels, and point of purchase. These items play an integral part in the retail experience, and designers have made innovative use of print and production finishes in the successful formulation of persuasive solutions. Shopping has become one of the developed world's most popular pastimes, and buying into the right brands is perceived as saying much about a purchaser's lifestyle and ambition. The use of a broad spectrum of print finishes, production techniques, and materials has produced a diverse and inspiring range of promotional items that come together to help a shopper choose what to buy within highly competitive product arenas.

The submissions for this book demonstrate that, by exploring the scope of materials and processes, designers are creating solutions that work hard to send numerous complex messages to as many existing and potential consumers as possible. Designers are assessing the brand, its market, and a project's print and production budget in order to tempt consumers to make associations that define not only contexts, but also an individual's personal style and aspirations.

There are many messages that can be created visually through the use of print finishes, production techniques, and materials. Visually interesting and tactile printed surfaces, varieties of material, and carefully selected techniques all have the potential to establish connections within the viewer's mind of, for example, environment, culture, exclusivity, craftsmanship, gender, and age. To successfully communicate these complex messages by text alone would probably require an excessively wordy description. Visual language created by using a mix of print and production techniques and materials is a very efficient way of communicating brand character, appeal, and positioning; it is not only quickly assimilated, but also easily crosses many cultural and language boundaries. As David Crow suggests:

"The ability of images to communicate across linguistic boundaries offers a level of consistency that is difficult to achieve otherwise. It also has distinct cost advantages. In a global economy, the ability to distribute the same product in a number of territories saves both time and money."[1]

By combining materials and processes, the connotations of differing qualities and characteristics impact upon one another to create a fascinating synergy of meanings. Contrasting materials can come together to depict very distinctive styles and messages, which often appeal to quite focused target markets. For example, a label printed on an elaborate combination of tough, hard-wearing fabric with a more feminine, intricate material, held together by a metallic component, can become representative of a particular type of youth culture or "style tribe." The graphic styling of the tags helps to categorize the product as much as the product itself does.

Advances in technology and transglobal production have allowed designers to produce cost-effective solutions, as well as being creatively ambitious and adventurous. No longer are designers restricted by printing presses with extremely limited operations; it is now possible to combine full color with other options such as varnish, fluorescents, and metallic inks, in a manner that was not economically feasible a few years ago.

Graphic designers can now utilize production procedures that were once used exclusively by other industries. This means that the palette of processes has widened considerably, encompassing influences including engineering, printed and constructed textiles, plastics, science, and ecology. Gone are the conventions that confined designers to solutions that simply involved traditional print on paper or board; competition now dictates that bag, label, and point-of-purchase design often has to embrace the broadening range of print and production processes in order to maintain brand positioning and profile.

The term "material" initially suggests a spectrum of products including paper, fabric, plastic, leather, and metal; however, it is important to recognize that within each of these categories there is a wealth of choice available. For example, there are many kinds of papers and boards that vary tremendously in terms of surface quality, texture, durability, resilience, and weight. Creating a bag in really heavyweight paper gives it an entirely different feel and character from one made in a lighter-weight stock; a wine label printed on textured paper will convey a totally different message from one printed on metallic paper. Combine or contrast these materials with carefully chosen print and production techniques, and the variations are endless. Gunther Kress and Theo van Leeuwen comment on the intricacies of meaning potential created by diverse choices of materials:

"The hastily torn-out scrap of paper has different sets of potentials as a signifier than does the beautifully made weighty sheet. Glossy paper has the possibility of signals of a different kind to matte—and here the complexities of materials as signifiers already appear: 'glossy' paper can serve as a signifier of value, and yet, in different contexts, it can also serve as the signifier of pretence of value."[2]

This book investigates the print and production finishes used within three distinct graphic design specialisms: bags; tags and labels; and point-of-purchase design. Featured bag designs demonstrate how many different materials can make effective, practical, and sometimes very exciting carrying devices. On occasions, the materials are sourced from extremely unusual and unexpected arenas that include carpet fitting and medicine; other times, more conventional materials are used, but print and finishing techniques combine to create different and desirable effects. Attention to detail in terms of handle materials or structures, stitching, die-cutting, or foil blocking, stands out as being highly effective in personalizing these practical marketing tools.

The graphic styling of labels shown in this book proves that they can heighten the appeal and market positioning of many varied products. Hangtags in particular convey a sense of value and individual care that is remarkable given their small scale. Add to this cleverly selected print and production processes, and products can be distinguished and elevated in a manner that is invaluable to marketing and sales.

Featured point-of-purchase designs show some of the effects created by the carefully considered use of print and production finishes, for both two- and three-dimensional promotional and display items. Point-of-purchase design particularly benefits from the use of unusual and memorable methods to attract interest, and clever combinations of different materials and processes can prove very successful in this quest for attention.

Print and Production Finishes for Bags, Labels, and Point of Purchase shows examples of a wide variety of processes in all three of these areas, and discusses the intriguing messages that help to define brand and personal image.

Notes > [1] Crow, David. *Left to Right: The Cultural Shift From Words to Pictures.* AVA Publishing SA, 2006.
[2] Kress, Gunther, and Theo van Leeuwen. *Reading Images: The Grammar of Visual Design.* Routledge, 1996.

STANDARD PRINTING

The work appearing in this section is printed by lithography, either in four-color or in a number of selected PANTONE colors. Lithography is the most common, practical, and economical print process for quantity runs of items displaying image and/or text. However, this does not mean that an alternative process would have been chosen had a client brief been different, or the budget higher. As the examples here show, standard lithography can be the very best method of printing many design solutions. In particular, color photography must be printed in four-color litho if images are to be represented showing all their subtle nuances of color, tone, and texture. Precision of type, right down to 5- or 6-point in size, is also achievable in lithography.

In the context of hangtags and carrier bags, full-color litho is especially significant, because very often these items are printed in a limited number of colors. Full color is therefore comparatively unusual, and can be used to connote certain messages to readers. For example, images with muted, tertiary hues can suggest that associated products, services, or environments are luxurious and expensive, whereas predominantly bright, vibrant, primary hues can evoke upmarket, lively, sporty, or youthful associations. Proportions and configurations of color impact upon visual language, but whatever the design, full-color lithography is unique in being able to convey a wide spectrum of meanings, as well as creating exciting and innovative hangtags and carrier bags.

Since the advent of sophisticated software that enables designers to manipulate images and type to create distinct impressions, characteristics, and styles, it could be said that there is less need for varying print processes and materials. For example, the RedHead hangtag shown on page 011 (designed by Matt Graif) is printed in four-color litho onto stiff board, and looks as if it is made up of a wooden base, with handmade paper layered on top, and an embossed metal emblem. In fact, all the effects have been produced and assembled on the computer, including the three-dimensional illusion, and it is likely that most viewers will barely make the distinction between this printed version and one constructed from the "raw" materials. Lithography has enabled all the inherent semantics of the combined materials to be produced very effectively and efficiently with just one process.

Litho printing in selected PANTONE colors, as opposed to colors from the four-color set, is also an excellent way to ensure continuity of identity for a range of printed items, and can often give more vibrant color. Specific PANTONE colors can be chosen as company or product colors and, providing they are consistently printed onto similar stock, they will always appear the same. Uniquely, lithography enables those PANTONE colors to mix and form other colors; two colors when printed in litho can overlap to form a third color, as the inks are not opaque. Images also can be manipulated in software to create duotones or tritones that mix two or three colors in assorted proportions to give a number of color variations.

In particular, this section on standard printing demonstrates the diversity and professional use of lithography. From small single-color labels to full-color point-of-purchase posters, the process is able to achieve high-quality image and text printed on a wide spectrum of paper stocks, and is often the very best process to choose.

LA PECA DE LUPE

DESIGN
SONSOLES LLORENS DISSENY GRAFIC

SPECIFICATIONS
■ Tag › three-color offset lithography
■ Paper bag › three-color offset lithography
■ Plastic bag › three-color flexography

This range, designed by Sonsoles Llorens for the La Peca de Lupe brand, features a tag and two types of carrier bag. Each is printed in three colors using a standard print method: either litho or flexography. Both types of print allow the designer to produce areas of consistent, crisp-edged, flat color. What is interesting to observe here is the differences in print effects that have been achieved simply printing the same colors onto different materials.

The tag is printed onto an absorbent uncoated stock, which causes the ink to sink in and results in a slight muting of color. The paper bag is also printed onto an uncoated stock, but on a bright white, lighter-weight, and less absorbent material that results in a slightly more vivid print quality. The plastic bag, which is printed using flexography, has a completely different effect; ink remains on the surface rather than being absorbed into the body of the bag. Overall, the print and production processes used throughout these three pieces help to reinforce the impression that La Peca de Lupe is a contemporary brand that appeals to a predominantly young-at-heart, female market.

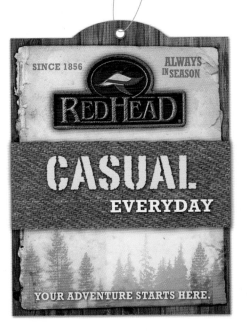

LABELS

REDHEAD

DESIGN
MATT GRAIF DESIGN

SPECIFICATIONS
- Four-color process
- One special PANTONE color

Many designers of labels and swingtags layer materials in an intriguing way to create a specific meaning that will appeal to a particular market. In these examples, Matt Graif has created a similarly complex, three-dimensional layered effect, but has used four-color process plus one special to achieve this result.

RedHead adventure gear has a range of three labels: cold-weather hunting clothes, everyday casual clothes, and field-tested footwear. The label for each line cleverly creates the illusion that it is made from three layers of material—a thin wooden board, a piece of deckle-edged handmade paper, and a wraparound label that appears to be made from material appropriate to each range. Camouflage fabric denotes hunting; denim defines the casual range; and brown leather indicates footwear. In reality, this effect has been achieved with the aid of litho printing in five colors, yet it still succeeds in communicating quite complex messages to the audience. For example, it is clear that the RedHead range appeals mainly to men, and the use of litho printing (as opposed to the more costly alternative of hand-fixing three different materials together) will assure the brand's customers that they are getting good value for money when purchasing a RedHead garment.

BAG

CROATIAN NATIONAL TOURIST BOARD

DESIGN
STUDIO INTERNATIONAL/HTZ

SPECIFICATIONS
▮ Four-color lithography

This design samples long stripes of colorful detail, sourced from Croatian imagery, and is expertly printed in CMYK to capture the contrasting individuality of these many shades, hues, and textures. The visual language created by the selection and use of four-color print speaks primarily of variety, while the choice of imagery also encompasses meanings such as heritage and enviably beautiful environments.

GALERIE AU CHOCOLAT

DESIGN
PAPRIKA

SPECIFICATIONS
▮ Four-color lithography

Paprika's labels for Galerie au Chocolat indicate the product details cleanly and have great visual impact on the shelf. Designs were printed in four-color litho and make full use of the potential of this process. This includes the creation of specific full-color mixes to capture individual shades; the accurate reproduction of photographic imagery; and the printing of subtle, tinted background shades. With this printing method, all this can happen at the same time, using only four passes on press.

CALISTOGA BAKERY CAFE

014

DESIGN
VRONTIKIS DESIGN OFFICE

SPECIFICATIONS
- Labels > three-color lithography
- Bags > four-color flexography, lamination

The distinctive, rich, earthy color palette remains consistent throughout every separate element that makes up Vrontikis Design Office's work for the Calistoga Bakery Cafe, yet each standalone item features well-considered and varied use of shifting color priority. Bags and labels are printed using two standard methods, depending upon which material is to be printed: paper-based products have been created using lithography, whereas silky-smooth, laminated foil coffee bags are produced using the most suitable process for their surface—flexography. These bags are first printed in white to provide a base that will enhance the quality of the remaining colors.

The selection of three PANTONE colors has provided the Calistoga Bakery Cafe with considerable design scope with which to differentiate their products. Each color has sufficient depth and density to hold even small serif typography without compromising legibility. The basic palette of red, yellow, and brown is occasionally supplemented with deep blue, but the design still remains true to the economy and visual character created by the three-color print palette.

The complementary combination of earthy
shades, simply yet beautifully printed in litho and
flexography, blends fluidly with the varied color
priority. This not only helps add significant value
to Calistoga Bakery Cafe products, but also helps
to reinforce the impression that product and service
possess the same degree of quality, consideration,
care, and attention to detail that is present within
the design.

STAVERTON

DESIGN
FORM

SPECIFICATIONS
▌ Lithography
▌ Die-cutting

Staverton uses a distinctive set of vivid corporate colors, the most characteristic being a bright, lively yellow, which has been recognized and exploited to the full by design company Form in the creation of these two carrier bags. Litho printing enabled precise color matching on each bag, with Staverton yellow even appearing within the sunny landscape of the smaller carrier and being used as a major source of corporate recognition on the outside of the larger bag. Yellow is usually perceived as bright and uplifting, and the Landscape bag makes a feature of the picturesque yellow-flowering crops that are evident in many rural environments. The designer is suggesting that "roomscapes," including Staverton furniture, have a similarly edifying effect.

INVITATION LABELS

COLORGRAPHICS

DESIGN
BELYEA

SPECIFICATIONS
- Four-color lithography
- Adhesive stock
- Metal eyelets

The only way to successfully achieve "true" full-color print on the surface of textured, colored stock is to print onto another medium, such as sticky labeling, and then adhere the printed material to the textured paper. Printing four-color process straight onto colored, uncoated stock can result in the print taking on an unwanted hue, and possibly compromising the sharpness of the print. This was exactly the situation facing Belyea when it was designing ColorGraphics art invitations; the covers use a mix of tactile, uncoated board in various shades, and small, fine text and subtly detailed full-color imagery had to be accommodated without any compromise in quality. This was achieved by hand-positioning full-color adhesive labels on each cover. This process has added to the prestige of each invitation and, along with the overall choice of specialist textured paper and metal eyelets, enhances and complements the subject of the exhibitions.

LOUISE CARRIER GRAPHIC DESIGN

DESIGN
LOUISE CARRIER GRAPHIC DESIGN

SPECIFICATIONS
▪ Two-color lithography

Louise Carrier created a striking design using two colors—black and cyan. These were litho-printed onto a versatile crack-back label material, and cleverly used to inject her house style and colors into a variety of situations. The label is shown neatly folding over and sealing the opening of brown kraft-paper carrier bags to form an extremely cost-effective packaging and promotional solution; this stylishly customizes plain, off-the-shelf brown bags, turning them into a desirable must-have accessory and sales tool. The labels can also be used to personalize letterheads, envelopes, parcels, and bespoke items. The simplicity of the design and production signals handmade, design-aware exclusivity to the viewer.

Shifting color priority and varied use of tints expands
the range and possible uses of these two-color labels
without increasing the print or production costs.

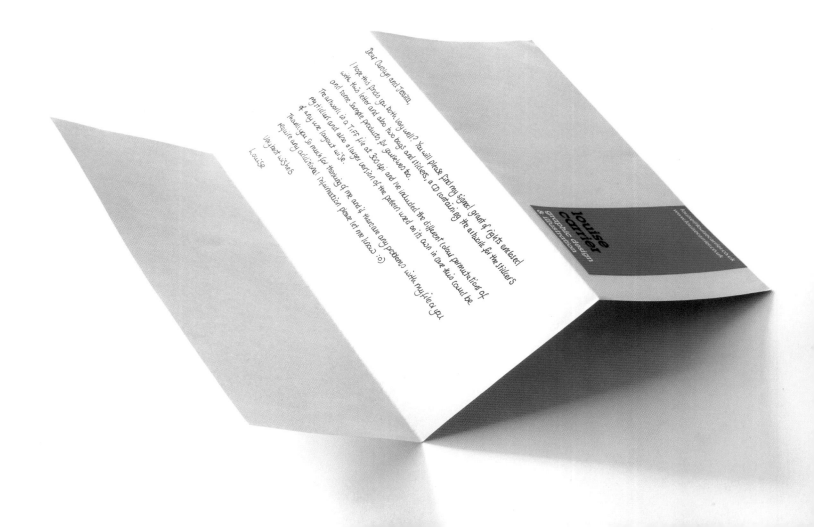

IOWA STATE FAIR

DESIGN
SAYLES GRAPHIC DESIGN

SPECIFICATIONS
▪ Three- and four-color lithography
▪ Kraft-paper bags

Iowa-based design company Sayles has a long-running history of designing marketing material for the annual Iowa State Fair. The selection featured on these pages provides an overview of the lively results that have been achieved with the simple use of offset printing with PANTONE colors onto kraft-paper bags. This printing method, combined with long-term consistent use of material and colors, has become a distinctive and memorable feature of the fair in recent years, and has helped to reinforce the excitement, fun, and vitality of the event.

The 2004 bag (shown left) involves particularly fascinating use of print, as it was produced using three PANTONE colors, but appears to use more. Sayles has carefully specified overprinting and the use of duotone, tritone, and lightly tinted halftone images in order to successfully extend the possibilities of this color palette.

By mixing two of the deepest featured colors, a shade perceived as "nearly black" was achieved. Certain duotones were created by varying the balance of the two selected and combined PANTONE shades, which produced a variety of surprisingly different results.

The use of overprinting, duotones, and tritones is an excellent way of economically extending the color possibilities of designs that are to be litho-printed in two or three shades. Colors can be made to work hard, and the end result can be far more interesting, as well as appearing far more exclusive and costly than it really is.

MAKE FEET BEAUTIFUL POINT OF PURCHASE

DESIGN
INKSURGE

SPECIFICATIONS
▌ Four-color lithography
▌ Laser printing

Inksurge's characteristic illustrative style is used here within a point-of-purchase display for Make Feet Beautiful. The four-color print process was adopted in both laser and offset-litho printing in order to accommodate the wide spectrum of colors as well as the variety of materials. Surface designs for shoe uppers were laser-printed in full color onto canvas. The fabric was then cut out and made into espadrilles, which in turn fixed to the wall by their soles. The poster that complements this footwear display is offset-litho printed.

BARCELONA ENERGY AGENCY

DESIGN
SONSOLES LLORENS DISSENY GRAFIC

SPECIFICATIONS
▪ Three-color offset lithography

The Barcelona Energy Agency bag is printed in three PMS offset litho, to enable Sonsoles Llorens to produce large, eye-catching areas of flat, intense color. This design features yellow and two bright oranges (which are always difficult to achieve out of the four-color set). It was superbly printed on a bright white paper bag to connote the clean, sustainable energy with which the agency is concerned.

COVET FURNITURE

DESIGN
PALAZZOLO DESIGN

SPECIFICATIONS
▪ Single-color lithography
▪ Adhesive stock
▪ Die-cutting

Simple, one-color printing on adhesive labeling was used to introduce a new colorway to Covet Furniture's binder in a cost effective way. The circular, blue die-cut label was applied to the spine of Palazzolo Design's hand-stenciled black-and-white folder to create a dramatic and colorful contrast to the characteristic soft, blurred edges of the stenciling.

Adhesive labeling proves time and again to be a simple, flexible, and effective way of introducing information and color into a design, without going to great expense.

UNAVAILABLE

DESIGN
SAGMEISTER, INC.

SPECIFICATIONS
▪ Single-color lithography

Sagmeister, Inc. used single-color label printing to great effect in its design for Unavailable perfume. Black labels were printed on both sides and carefully positioned onto the front and rear of the perfume bottles, so that when viewed from certain positions, the fronts of the labels obscure the writing on the inside of the rear labels. The text that is covered up is "UNAVAILABLE," making this design a clever visual metaphor.

CONTENTS

It is uncommon to find labels with information printed directly below adhesive, but as long as these stickers are adhered to a transparent surface, print information will be perfectly legible.

NEIMAN MARCUS

DESIGN
STEVEN WILSON

SPECIFICATIONS
▌ Four-color lithography

Brightly colored line drawings set against a dramatic, contrasting black background create very exciting and stylish promotional bags, postcards, and gift cards in this 2005 in-store promotion for Neiman Marcus.

Full color has been exploited to best effect with each hue being formed from only two colors from the CMYK process. This gives the printing a purity and clarity, enabling a special vibrancy to be achieved; more colors are inclined to "muddy" the colorful effect.

The sophisticated design and print interpretation produces a vivacious style while maintaining high-end market appeal. The linear illustrations create a sensitively balanced proportional relationship between image and background, and this allows an effective combination of vitality and finesse.

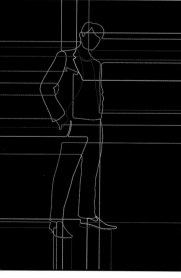

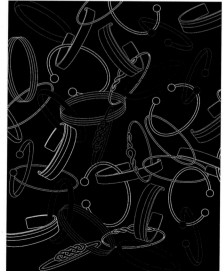

The glossy surface of the carrier bag heightens the impact of the linear color against black, and adds the interplay of reflections to the distinct visual character of this Neiman Marcus promotion.

BREEDER'S CHOICE ADVANCED PET DIETS

DESIGN
SHIMOKOCHI-REEVES

SPECIFICATIONS
▌ Labels > three-color lithography
▌ Bags > four-color flexography

Two common PANTONE colors were printed using completely different processes within Shimokochi-Reeves' designs for Advanced Pet Diets. Labels were printed using conventional three-color litho, while bags were printed using four-color flexography. Both of these products, designed to sit next to each other on the supermarket shelf, share two colors—PMS 3435 and PMS 185—with other colors changing to signify different varieties. It is interesting to note that, even side by side, it is difficult to observe a difference in the print quality.

   These carefully considered and executed print methods combine with the chosen color scheme and design to convince the purchaser that Advanced Pet Diets offer a scientifically tested, high-quality range of wholesome pet foods for every stage of an animal's life.

PESCAIA WINE

DESIGN
GIORGIO DAVANZO DESIGN

SPECIFICATIONS
■ Four-color lithography
■ Uncoated paper

"Facelli Winery makes hand-crafted wine, and in order to communicate these values to the customer, I chose to use a full-color simulation of letterpress printing," says designer Giorgio Davanzo of these labels.

The success and interest of their design owes much to the close evocation of letterpress printing. In reality, a design this colorful would be very complicated to achieve using this historical printing method, as each individual, brightly colored letter would have to be separately inked up and printed. Consequently, Giorgio Davanzo's solution is a practical and cost-effective method of achieving a very similar result while reinforcing messages associated with craftsmanship and quality.

030

SANS & SANS

DESIGN
SONSOLES LLORENS DISSENY GRAFIC

SPECIFICATIONS
▌ Labels > single-color lithography, adhesive white stock
▌ Carrier bags > single-color lithography

Sonsoles Llorens designed a range of two-part single-color labels and carrier bags for Sans & Sans fine tea merchants; each item from this range was economically printed using single-color litho.

Silver tea caddies are sealed with long, thin, blue labels. The front of each container features a circular label, again printed in single color, but this time a color chosen to reflect a specific variety of tea. Each label fully exploits the possibilities of printing detailed halftone imagery, which is shown as background illustration and includes a great variety of tone. The bright white of the adhesive labeling is also used to good effect; typographic detail is shown reversed through the single-color print, in effect expanding the Sans & Sans color palette even further, for no extra cost.

Bags are also printed in single-color blue litho, and again make extensive use of the possibilities created by printing halftone imagery. These sturdy paper bags, together with their broad cotton handles, have been carefully chosen to reinforce the quality and nature of this "boutique" brand.

The print used for both designs works hard, and creates a range of tonal variations to add considerable interest and detail to these pieces.

BAGS

THE CHILDREN'S GENERAL STORE

DESIGN
ALEXANDER ISLEY INC.

SPECIFICATIONS
▪ Flexography
▪ White paper bags

These bags, featuring a simple, hand-drawn harlequin pattern, were printed using flexography. "We wanted to establish a strong visual presence that would be easy to print and look just as good using a variety of printing processes—hence the hand-drawn repeat pattern," explains Alexander Isley.

The patterning and color scheme is also carried through to co-ordinated tissue paper. The combination of print, design, and material helps to inform the viewer of the fun to be had when purchasing an item from The Children's General Store, and also succeeds in conveying a sense of responsibility and quality.

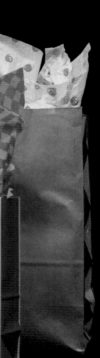

BATH HOUSE SPANISH FIG & NUTMEG RANGE

DESIGN
BATH HOUSE

SPECIFICATIONS
▌Two- and four-color lithography
▌Ribbon

Signature colors of black, warm white, and reddish-brown are taken from the ribbon that is included in all of the labeling for Bath House's Spanish Fig & Nutmeg range. The self-adhesive labels are printed in black and brown in two-color litho onto warm white paper. The hangtags, although appearing to be two-color brown and black, are in fact printed four-color to bring out the richness and depth of the landscape image.

Long, narrow adhesive labels wrap around the tops of these packs, with ribbon secured by either end of the labels continuing around the bases. In all of the card and paper packaging, the ribbon is an integral part of the labeling; as paper and ribbon combine to completely encircle each product, they create an attractive, yet masculine identity.

Bath House demonstrates attention to detail by printing the hangtag on the Spanish Fig & Nutmeg Bath Soak in full color. The remainder of the printing for this range is two-color, but there is no doubt that had the landscape been printed in brown alone, it would not have captured the atmosphere and depth Bath House deemed necessary to sell the product.

This close-up of the soap-bar label demonstrates the ability of lithography to represent the nuances of tonal change that distinguish typographic letterforms from handwriting. Both the illustration and ink-pen writing are printed in black as grayscale images, and it is hard to believe that the words "Glycerine, Nutmeg, Olive Oil, Fig" have not been added by hand to suggest to purchasers that the products are made on a small Spanish farm.

BAGS

PEOPLE ARE PEOPLE

DESIGN
INKSURGE

SPECIFICATIONS
▪ Four-color offset lithography
▪ Coated stock
▪ Gloss varnish

Inksurge printed distinctive illustrations on carrier bags for fashion store People are People. Gloss varnish was applied overall to give each bag a high-shine surface. By using the four-color process, all bags could be printed on the same print run and still have a distinctly focused color theme and a clear individuality.

Careful blending of combinations of cyan, magenta, yellow, and black has produced vivid shades of blue-green, pink, and yellow.

MUSLIMGAUZE REMIX

DESIGN
PLAZM MEDIA, INC.

SPECIFICATIONS
▌Single-color lithography

One of the most cost-effective methods of printing is single-color litho using black ink, and this is exactly what Plazm used in its label design for Muslimgauze Remix's. The design is printed on coated white stock, and shows white through a solid black background. One of the most striking elements of the design is the fact that it is wrapped around a contrasting golden fur-fabric background, creating the impression that the music contained within the pack is distinctive, individual, and surprising.

XTZ INDUSTIES X-DRINX

DESIGN
TRAIN OF THOUGHT

SPECIFICATIONS
- Four-color lithography
- Varnish

It is amazing how bright color can appear when printed from the four-color set; by carefully considering precise color mixes, compositions, and locations, hues can seem almost fluorescent. For example, it is possible for 100% cyan with just the smallest touch of yellow to be almost as bright as fluorescent blue, especially if positioned next to another color of the same visual temperature. This ultra-vivid, almost oscillating, effect—created out of four-color print—was used to great advantage within the design of X-Drinx labels, giving each variety an energetic, lively appearance that echoes the energy-giving qualities of the drink itself.

RED CAR WINE COMPANY

DESIGN
VRONTIKIS DESIGN OFFICE

SPECIFICATIONS
▪ Four-color lithography
▪ Uncoated stock

Excellent-quality four-color litho captures the subtleties of the illustrations that theme the Red Car Wine Company labels. The distinctive label for each vintage is used to perpetuate a long-running story that is portrayed using a specialist style of illustration. Within the featured label for The Table, scanning and print have captured the subtleties of changes in depth created by the original collaged illustration. This conjures a tactile quality that suggests to potential purchasers that the wine is not only handmade, but also hand-labeled, especially for their individual enjoyment.

THE FEAREY GROUP

DESIGN
BELYEA

SPECIFICATIONS
▪ Wine labels › four-color lithography, on-roll labeling, die-cutting
▪ Tags › three-color lithography, uncoated stock

The label and swingtag featured on this page were produced using good-quality, standard litho print utilizing a consistent group of colors; in fact, the best possible economy of print was achieved, as Belyea printed the Fearey Group gift tags at the same time as the group's business cards. This is a practical solution to the need to produce two items.

Belyea carefully considered the Fearey Group's distinctive corporate color palette to ensure that when printing on two different materials (uncoated stock and roll-based adhesive labeling), the litho-printed results matched. Printing with special PANTONE colors allows the effective and subtle use of tints—as shown on this gift tag—and effectively introduces the impression of another, related color without any extra cost.

By producing a two-part wine label using bespoke colors that match the foil capsule and ribbon, Belyea created the impression of high-quality vintage wine. This visual message is, of course, carefully managed to ensure that wine recipients also associate these qualities with the Fearey Group.

BATH HOUSE GARDENER'S BATH SOAK

DESIGN
BATH HOUSE

SPECIFICATIONS
▌Two-color lithography

A very strong and comparatively cost-effective identity has been accomplished for this product by selecting a dark brown glass bottle and printing both the label and hangtag in two-color lithography, using warm black and orange on white stock. Lithography brings out the subtleties of tone in the halftone images, and complements them with a clear, solid orange that is notoriously difficult to achieve in four-color printing. The choice of colors and images, as well as the character of the printing, ensures that this product appeals to male and female gardeners.

Warm black produces tints of brown, so the grayscale image of a white flower has lovely warm shadows when printed on white paper. As a solid, it matches the glass bottle, and almost makes the flower, type, and orange bar appear as if they were printed directly onto the bottle itself.

VINTAGE PEANUTS

DESIGN
MSLK

SPECIFICATIONS
▮ Four-color lithography

The spirit of this clothing line seeks to capture the essence of the Peanuts brand from 1962 to 1968. Emotionally, the graphics are intended to make the viewer feel as if they are wearing a well-loved sweatshirt or a pair of jeans that are slightly worn around the edges. Although the hangtag is printed in regular four-color offset litho to create a believable vintage feel, MSLK produced printouts of label designs, then crumpled and physically distressed them before scanning the resulting weathered and "aged" effect for the artwork. The four-color process, printed on an absorbent, uncoated stock, has successfully captured the subtleties of the color scheme and textures of vintage labeling.

The designers at MSLK used Photoshop to create the slightly misregistered feel of the Snoopy and Woodstock illustrations, with background color and texture being enhanced by including a larger than normal dot-screen pattern. Using litho printing on absorbent, uncoated stock, these print effects cleverly conjure the less refined printing of Peanuts cartoons back in the 1960s.

RED CAR
WINE COMPANY

DESIGN
VRONTIKIS DESIGN OFFICE

SPECIFICATIONS
▌Three-color lithography

This Vrontikis Design Office label, produced for the Red Car Wine Company, was printed using three-color litho, and features careful color selection and matching. Think Pink Rosé has a very distinctive color, which is highly visible through the clear glass bottle, and this product characteristic has been the foundation of color selection for label printing. Specially selected vivid pink and orange were printed evenly in litho. Each color is shown separately, but sitting side by side, allowing potential purchasers to subconsciously recognize Think Pink's freshness, flavor, and quality. A mix of these two colours produces the beautifully luminous hue of the product.

044

RYDERS EYEWEAR

DESIGN
SUBPLOT DESIGN INC.

SPECIFICATIONS
▪ Boxes > four-color lithography, die-cutting
▪ Posters > four-color process

Subplot has very skillfully designed Ryders Eyewear boxes to double as both packaging and point-of-sale material. Printing in full color has allowed the designers to capture, in photographs, how this performance eyewear stands up to the rigors of the consumers' lifestyle. Each box and poster shows a close-cropped portrait of a sportsperson wearing Ryders, and images are set against contrasting black backgrounds.

Although the images are almost monochrome, full-color printing has achieved a depth, intensity, and richness, particularly in the background.

After printing, the boxes were die-cut and folded, then configured in dynamic groups to create individual point-of-purchase displays.

VITAMIN

DESIGN
MORROW MCKENZIE DESIGN

SPECIFICATIONS
▊ Two- and four-color lithography

Simple two- and four-color litho labels were designed by Morrow McKenzie for these Vitamin packs, with the shapes of the labels echoing each unconventionally shaped pack. One of the most unusual elements of this design is the manner in which the labels have been applied; they are adhered to the lower part of each pack, extending round onto the base. This proves that even the simplest design produced economically can be used to achieve a very striking, contemporary effect.

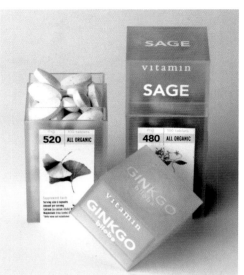

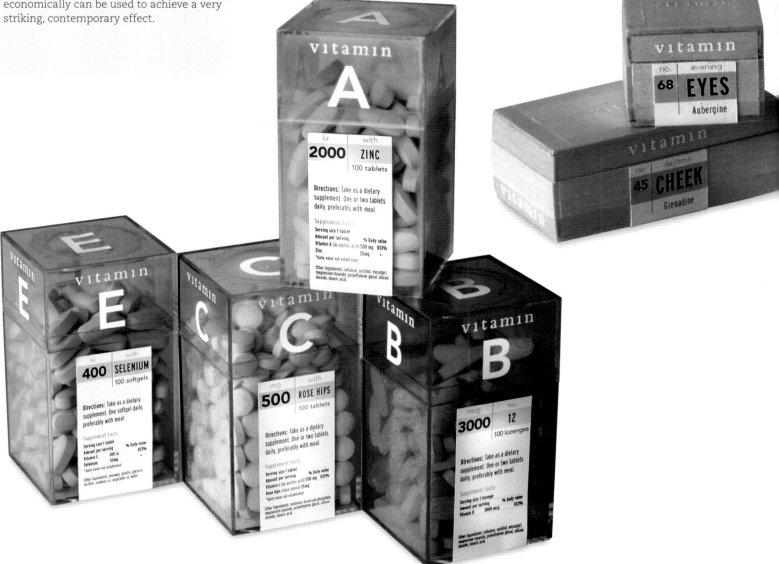

RIVER TOWN FOODS
GIRLY SAUCES

DESIGN
MATT GRAIF DESIGN

SPECIFICATIONS
▪ Four-color lithography
▪ White adhesive labeling

This Girly Sweet & Sassy BBQ Sauce label
is printed using the four-color process
onto white adhesive-label material. The
predominant colors in this design are pink,
brown, and black, but designer Matt Graif
has specified full color in order to ensure
maximum depth of tone and richness,
particularly within areas such as the
illustration and textured backgrounds.
To most viewers, it appears as a three-
color identity with an unusual, individual,
and slightly quirky style.

ESSIE COSMETICS

DESIGN
STORMHOUSE PARTNERS

SPECIFICATIONS
▪ Two-color lithography
▪ Gloss label stock

To ensure clear, pure hues, the lighter shades of these two-color labels are separate PANTONE colors. "Essie has a certain elegance to its products and brand," says Rodney Dirso of Stormhouse Partners. "The challenge was bringing this feeling to such a low-budget project." Using a serif typeface and carefully controlled layout, plus two PMS colors printed on gloss labels, Stormhouse Partners has achieved the desired effect.

Very often, for reasons of economy, designs that include two shades of the same hue are printed using a solid PANTONE color together with a percentage tint of this color. In the case of these Essie cosmetics labels, the shades are printed in two separate, solid PANTONE colors, providing a subtle difference that upholds the company's quality and attention to detail.

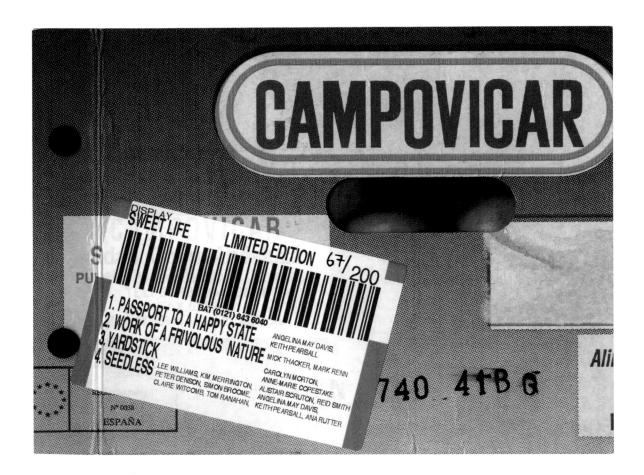

BIRMINGHAM ART TRUST: SWEET LIFE

DESIGN
BOING!

SPECIFICATIONS
■ Two-color lithography
■ Adhesive labeling

With an exhibition catalog cover made from recycled fruit boxes, what could be a more appropriate way of imposing titling and content detail than a two-color label, designed and printed to exactly mimic the style of supermarket labeling? Boing! has undertaken a considerable amount of research to source the exact detailing that would be used for this item—down to ensuring that the label is adhered to the cover at just the right jaunty angle. The printers created an authentic barcode which, when scanned, reveals the message "sweet life."

Catalog recipients are bound to recognize that Boing! has created an item of intriguing fascination and beauty from what appears to be totally recycled materials. These properties are likely to be associated with the exhibition, thus increasing visitor interest and numbers.

SPECIALIST PRINTING

Specialist printing, for the purposes of this book, covers screen printing, laser/inkjet printing, web-offset printing, the use of rubber stamps, and printing with varnish, metallics, and pastels. In each instance, the printing method was selected either for its particular effect, or because of the material on which it is being printed. All methods covered within this section use exclusive inks and substances that have different visual characteristics, and therefore tend to produce distinctive visual messages.

Screen printing most commonly utilizes very opaque inks that block out any paper or ink color from underneath. This produces powerful, flat areas of color that stand slightly proud of the print surface, and enables areas of white or pale color, both as shapes or type, to be printed onto darker stock.

Items that the designer wishes to appear individual are quite frequently screen-printed. The process involves squeezing the ink through the unblanked-out areas of silk stretched onto a frame; this means that each item is unique, as it is impossible to apply each color identically every time. The inevitability of all items being unique is very pleasing and desirable. Even without knowing the practicalities of the process, the visual quality of silk-screen printing has the ability to evoke a handcrafted, "one-off" character that communicates the individuality of a product or company. An excellent example of this print process is Dotzero's bag design on page 068. Areas of matte opaque inks sit pleasingly on the slightly shiny surface of good-quality brown paper, in a manner that could not be achieved by any other method of printing.

Screen printing is also an appropriate method of applying line-based information to a range of materials, such as plastic, wood, and fabric, as the inks have sufficient substance to avoid sinking into the print surface.

Laser and inkjet printing are undertaken directly from the computer, and are ideal for smaller numbers or unconventional sizes of prints. High-quality professional prints that do not fade are now available, and, as examples in this book demonstrate, this can be an extremely practical form of printing. Laser and inkjet printing, however, have a recognizable visual character. When designers select either of these printing methods for commercial work, the resulting visual language can be used to portray a sense of economy, immediacy, and/or disposability. Increasingly, companies wish to express care and concern for the environment, or to appear moderate in their spending, and computer printouts are able to suggest this attitude, at least to some extent.

Rubber-stamp printing is another method that is very practical for small quantities of print, and also communicates a company, service, or product's responsibility to the environment. Text or image generated by a rubber stamp has to be hand-produced, and, by responding to a supply-and-demand production system, a minimum of waste can be ensured. The distinctive textural markmaking also creates a style that conveys handcrafted individualism, which can be very appropriate in the context of labels and hangtags. David Crow considers that:

"The roughly rendered typography of the rubber stamp gives it a gestural immediacy. It suggests the informal. We can almost sense the sound the stamp would make when the image was being made."

Flexography is used in the printing of brown corrugated boxes, flexible packaging including retail and shopping bags, food and hygiene bags and sacks, flexible plastics, and self-adhesive labels. Image and text are printed using flexible rubber plates in order to accommodate uneven and pliable surfaces, with spirit-based inks that dry fairly speedily. Although flexography used to be appropriate only for comparatively crude designs, modern platemaking technology has enabled detailed, fine, full-color work to be produced.

The contrast between shiny and matte surfaces is always visually exciting, and the use of spot varnish on a number of bags, tags, and point-of-purchase items in this section of the book creates some very interesting designs. The effects are subtle, often relying on brief glimpses of light catching the complementary surfaces, but they never fail to add that "wow" factor.

Specialist printing techniques are appropriate in many contexts, from instances where the designer wants to create a sense of individuality, to occasions when economy or a greater quantity of items is required. Throughout this section, designers have clearly been inspired by the creative possibilities of specialist print techniques, and have used them to maximize the surface aesthetic and impact of their concepts.

BWO

Temple Of Love The Club Mixes

Capitol RECORDS   Music from EMI

POSTER

CASTANETS: FIRST LIGHT'S FREEZE

DESIGN
THE SMALL STAKES

SPECIFICATIONS
▮ Two-color silk-screen printing

This double-page spread shows three fascinating examples of point-of-purchase posters. The Castanets poster was printed using two contrasting colors—dark brown and blue—on white stock. The poster is framed by images of overlapping leaves, printed using a coarse halftone screen to capture the tonal detail produced by light and shade. Halftone detail is difficult to capture using silk-screen printing; the quality of the screen must be carefully considered to ensure that the ink is able to pass through the screen effectively, without clogging.

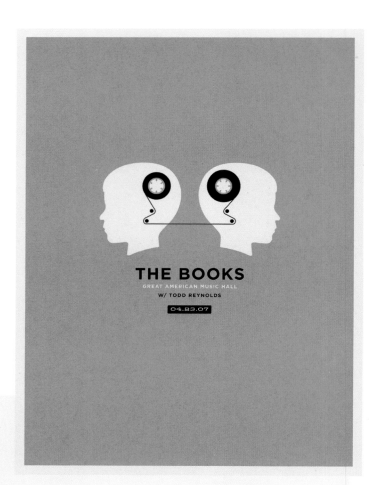

POSTER

THE BOOKS

DESIGN
THE SMALL STAKES

SPECIFICATIONS
▮ Two-color silk-screen printing

This poster is printed on off-white paper with metallic silver and black inks. Screen printing metallic inks tends to give a more truly metallic, glistening effect than is possible to achieve with litho inks alone, although the end result is affected by the quality of paper used. Coated papers provide a smoother, harder surface that is likely to achieve the most noticeably metallic effect, whereas uncoated papers are more absorbent and, to some degree, allow the ink to sink in, resulting in a more subtle metallic shimmer.

THE SHINS

27 MARCH 2007 at MANCHESTER ACADEMY

WWW.RICHARDGODDALLGALLERY.COM RGGI6O

POSTER

THE SHINS

DESIGN
THE SMALL STAKES

SPECIFICATIONS
▮ Three-color silk-screen printing

053

This Shins poster was printed with three opaque colors onto a minty green stock, which is significant as the ink used was specially selected to totally block out the color of the paper. This is a very useful property of screen printing, as it allows the designer to select a distinctive colored stock, and ensure that ink is going to sit on top of the selected material without being altered by it in any way. In this example, Jason Munn of The Small Stakes selected blue, brown, and white inks; there are very few print techniques that will allow the designer to "impose" white onto a design. The most common way of including white is to specify the use of white background stock, and to show this color reversed through the detail of a design.

PUMA SPRING/ SUMMER 07

DESIGN
RINZEN

SPECIFICATIONS
▌Large-scale digital output

Puma Stores have in-store display systems to take each new season's giant, digitally output, point-of-purchase imagery. Some images are presented with rear illumination, having first been printed onto specialist translucent film. Others simply slide into framing devices, after being printed onto high-quality laser paper. Large digital prints are an extremely cost-effective way of producing large-scale, limited-edition print runs, as images can be printed straight from artwork without the need for the costly platemaking necessary for lithographic printing. In addition, there are fewer restrictions on final print size, as digital printing presses come in a great range of sizes, and shorter print runs mean that, if necessary, prints can be tiled together or trimmed to achieve any desired size.

Many of the images for this Rinzen-designed point of purchase have cleverly used black backgrounds with centrally located areas of bright, vibrant color and white. This means that when back-illuminated, the light for the most part is blocked out by the dark areas and mainly shines through the brightly colored areas of organically shaped images, taking the viewer's attention away from the regular rectangular format of the display system.

HANGTAG

MOTH

DESIGN
IE DESIGN + COMMUNICATIONS

SPECIFICATIONS
▌ 2-PMS lithography including one metallic ink
▌ Die-cutting

The design choices within this label all help to communicate something visually about the name of the clothes store, Moth, and the vintage style of the garments it sells. Silver metallic ink is delightfully reminiscent of the iridescence of moth wings, as is the shape and structure of the curved die-cut foldover card. Off-white stock keys into the aged effect, and the litho metallic printing does not produce a solid silver character, but a more worn and antiqued image. According to the copy inside the tag, many clothes sold in Moth have frayed edges, uneven stitching, and torn lace; IE Design + Communications resisted the temptation to incorporate these elements into the label, and produced a more sophisticated, subtle design.

LABEL AND HANGTAG

MONTEZUMA'S

DESIGN
MONTEZUMA'S CHOCOLATES LTD.

SPECIFICATIONS
▮ Hot foil blocking
▮ Lithography
▮ Glossy transparent labeling
▮ Screen-printed ribbon

Transparent circular stickers have been printed with a distinctive silver hot foil "M" set against a matte blue star, and are used to seal clear cellophane bags containing Montezuma's gourmet chocolates. Bags are also labeled with two-color hangtags that are held in place with wide, screen-printed black ribbon, emphasizing the star-rated, award-winning styling that runs throughout the presentation of this quirky brand.

POINT OF PURCHASE

LEVI'S LADY STYLE

DESIGN
VAULT49/BBDO

SPECIFICATIONS
▍ Full-color laser printing

Levi's point-of-purchase designs by Vault49 and BBDO are evocative of stained-glass windows with biblical themes. These large-scale, dramatic images lend themselves well to specialist high-quality laser printing on translucent film, enabling the detail of the image to be seen while at the same time allowing bright white light to flood through and help to saturate colors.

These three designs are crammed full of tantalizing visual language, relating to Eve the temptress, provocatively wearing Levi's in her twenty-first-century Garden of Eden. The contemporary version of a stained-glass window, produced as a laser print, can only help to reinforce these erotic messages.

ALAGUA

DESIGN
SONSOLES LLORENS DISSENY GRAFIC

SPECIFICATIONS
▮ Two-color screen printing
▮ PVC
▮ Lithography
▮ 350gsm uncoated board

This is an example of a design that could happily find a home in more than one section of this book, but this tag appears in the specialist printing section because it was designed around the effects created by using two-color screen printing. The label is created in two parts: the rear element is simply cut from a mid-gray, textured, uncoated stock, while the front-facing label uses a clear sheet of PVC screen-printed on the reverse to create a smooth, highly shiny surface. When you print on the back of transparent material, information must be printed in reverse for it to be read correctly from the front.

This design, combined with its use of materials and processes, successfully appeals to the intended market of young women, as it conveys a strong, contemporary style.

MBG & SDS: NEW JACK

DESIGN
ZION GRAPHICS

SPECIFICATIONS
▋ Two-color lithography including silver

Zion Graphics designed a number of labeling devices for MBG & SDS. This disk has a two-color label, expertly printed in silver and pink. Zion also used die-cut holes in the outer sleeve, positioned to ensure that the interior album labeling plays a vital role in the exterior sleeve image. Stuck to the top right-hand corner of this sleeve is a two-color adhesive label, providing a platform for record details.

   This is an interesting and cost-effective alternative to printing directly onto the sleeve and, by using the same colors as on the record, this outer label unifies the entire design.

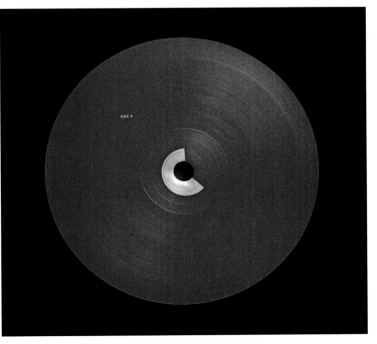

STICKERS AND BAG

BIRDHEAD

DESIGN
PRANK DESIGN

SPECIFICATIONS
- Organic cotton bag
- Silk-screen printing
- Water-based inks
- Vinyl stickers
- Four-color process

Perpetuating Birdhead's philosophy of creating with less waste, Prank has designed an organic cotton silk-screened bag to accommodate a sticker-adorned, full-color catalog. The bag is interesting for its use of organic cotton; it is likely to be retained and reused by recipients, and have a much longer life than a paper-based envelope. However, add to this silk-screen printing with water-based inks, and Prank's design really creates maximum impact, while having a minimal effect upon the environment.

The catalog contained within this bag is adorned with a number of vinyl adhesive labels, each of which has been hand-positioned so that copies of the catalog are bespoke and individual—thus echoing Birdhead's approach to clothing design. The catalog is litho-printed on recycled stock in full color using soya-based inks. The visual language of this design speaks of avant-garde individuality. It appeals to an environmentally conscious, style-aware youth market.

www.aGaiNnyC.cOM

aGaiN
(fRoM JunK tO FuNk)

This one-of-a-kind product is made from rescued and repurposed materials (JunK) and transformed into a stylish, practical accessory for modern life (FuNk).

Environmentally and socially conscious, aGaiN products are made in the USA and a portion of our profits are donated to environmental charities.

TieD uP in KNoTs YoGa bAg

AGAIN

DESIGN
MSLK

SPECIFICATIONS
 Hand printing with a rubber stamp

MSLK's design for aGaiN hangtags uses off-the-shelf, economically priced manila tags, printed using a specially created rubber stamp and opaque pigment stamp inks. This approach allows the labels to be customized for limited-quantity print runs while reinforcing aGaiN's attitude to sustainability and the environment.

"This company uses rescued and repurposed materials (junk) and transforms them into stylish, practical accessories for modern life (funk)—providing an excellent example of selected print and production finishes being used as a direct reflection of a company's own production processes and philosophies," comments Sheri Koetting, Principal of MSLK.

POSTER WITH LABELS

30 ARTISTS UNDER 40 EXHIBITION

DESIGN
R2 DESIGN

SPECIFICATIONS
▍Single-color label printing

R2's poster for the 30 Artists Under 40 exhibition held at Oslo's Stenersen Museum used printing onto adhesive labels on a roll. R2 designed a basic poster that can be customized by the addition of simple single-color labels, randomly hand-positioned to create individual poster designs. These labels, each containing a different message, are printed in black onto single-color yellow, then lightly tacked onto the posters to give a slightly three-dimensional appearance. R2 used sticky labels to capture some of the visual language of supermarkets, and to produce effective original posters.

065

BOXES

ASCOT SHOES BAMBOO

DESIGN
STUDIO OUTPUT

SPECIFICATIONS
▌ Four-color process
▌ High-gloss varnish
▌ Die-cutting

Studio Output designed this range of stackable boxes as a point-of-purchase piece for Ascot Shoes' Bamboo A. Each box was printed in full color, with an overall high-gloss varnish applied. The combination of vivid color, large areas of black, and (most importantly) this highly shiny, varnished surface, gives the viewer an impression of contemporary luxury with an oriental twist—the intention of the varnish is to recall the style of the intricate, oriental lacquered boxes.

Post-printing, the flat form of each box was die-cut out of board.

CAFFÈ ARTIGIANO

DESIGN
SUBPLOT DESIGN INC.

SPECIFICATIONS
- Coffee bags > four-color process, matte varnish, foil bags
- Labels > four-color lithography

Family-owned Caffè Artigiano produces and markets 16 varieties of artisan coffee, each of which is individually labeled with a full-color label design. The labels feature a selection of family photographs, each telling a different story. Although originally black-and-white, each image is printed in full color to provide a quality that reflects the age and character of old, treasured photos. Labels could easily have been printed using three special colors, but the print quality of photographic imagery would have been severely compromised, so four-color litho was selected.

Bags are also printed in four-color, then finished with a coating of matte varnish in order to provide a pleasingly smooth, tactile surface.

067

ODDITY CARDS

DESIGN
DOTZERO DESIGN

SPECIFICATIONS
▮ Two-color silk-screen printing

To most designers, a heavyweight brown paper bag is an item of beauty evoking a bygone age of quality and attention to detail. Dotzero Design utilized them as a starting point for packaging their latest self-promotion, screen printing each bag with two colors. The inks have a distinct matte quality that forms a memorable contrast with the sheen of brown paper. This design makes effective use of the contrast by building color and sheen into the detail of retro illustration. Dotzero Design selected silk screen as the method of printing, as the inks produce precise areas of quality, opaque color which would be impossible to achieve with any other printing method.

TITTERINGTON'S SCONES

DESIGN
SHEAFF DORMAN PURINS

SPECIFICATIONS
▊ Eight-color flexography
▊ Clear lamination
▊ Die-cutting

Sheaff Dorman Purins used complex eight-color flexography to print labels for Titterington's scones. Four-color process inks, plus four PANTONE specials, build up an elaborate color palette for these labels and help to reinforce the mildly eccentric, "folklore" brand image established by the style and content of the illustration and traditional serif typography. Post-printing, labels were laminated and die-cut into a triangular shape, adding two finishing processes to the already extravagant print specification for this job.

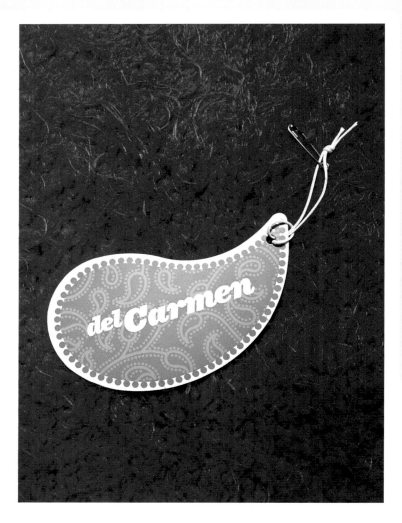

DEL CARMEN

DESIGN
SONSOLES LLORENS DISSENY GRAFIC

SPECIFICATIONS
▪ Two-color offset lithography
▪ One standard PANTONE color
▪ One fluorescent color
▪ Die-cutting

These del Carmen labels were printed using litho, but each version utilizes a combination of one standard PANTONE color and one fluorescent. Combining two colors with such joyful effect has created a sense of "visual electricity," with each color seeming to vibrate against the other. These energetic color combinations were selected to reflect the style of del Carmen clothing, which is made in India and inspired by contemporary Asian styles. The finished labels were die-cut into a shape derived from the simple illustrative style used throughout the range—the characteristic Indian almond motif.

BWO

Temple Of Love The Club Mixes

0946 358027 2 6. BIEM/n©b. bel/BIEM.
Made in EU. LC 0542. ℗ 2006 EMI Music
Sweden AB. © 2006 EMI Music Sweden
AB. All rights of the producer and of the
owner of the recorded work reserved.
Unauthorized copying, hiring, renting,
public performance and broadcasting of
this record prohibited. This label copy
information is the subject of copyright
protection. All rights reserved. © 2006
EMI Music Sweden AB.

Capitol RECORDS   Music from EMI

LABEL

BWO: TEMPLE OF LOVE

DESIGN
ZION GRAPHICS

SPECIFICATIONS
▮ Single-color screen printing

Zion Graphics has chosen to produce
quite a small area of labeling for BWO's
Temple of Love CD. The design is well
integrated with, and meets the curve
of the CD's edge. The labeling, which is
printed directly onto the surface of the
disc, uses a single color—white—with the
type reversed through to reveal the surface
of the CD below. The overall design relies
on the holographic color scheme of the
plain CD surface around the label to
provide a crucial colorful element.

BWO: HALCYON DAYS

DESIGN
ZION GRAPHICS

SPECIFICATIONS
▮ Screen printing

The ability to print labeling directly onto CDs has opened up a multitude of design possibilities. However, the most striking part of Zion Graphics' labeling for BWO's *Halcyon Days* is the area of the labeling that has not been printed. The majority of the CD is covered with Ricky Tillblad's design, but two narrow horizontal lines running above and below the typographic information remain clear and unprinted, revealing the naked surface of the CD below.

The design surprises shown on these two pages are created by allowing light to become a significant element of the design. These CD labels tell the viewer that the music the discs hold will be surprising and contemporary; they also suggest to any potential purchaser that this sense of modern, minimal style and good taste is a part of their own character and lifestyle.

BWO

Halcyon Days | 0946 358916 2 1
BIEM/n©b. bel/BIEM. Made in EU. LC 0542.
℗2006 EMI Music Sweden AB. ©2006
EMI Music Sweden AB. All rights of the
producer and of the owner of the recorded
work reserved. Unauthorized copying,
hiring, renting, public performance and
broadcasting of this record prohibited. This
label copy information is the subject of
copyright protection. All rights reserved.
©2006 EMI Music Sweden AB. This Copy
Control logo is a trademark of IFPI and is
used under licence.

BIRKS JEWELERS

DESIGN
PAPRIKA

SPECIFICATIONS
- Two-color lithography
- Foil blocking
- Lamination
- Metal eyelets

Paprika requested two new PANTONE colors specifically for Birks' use. "Using bespoke colors gave the bag a high-end finish and sense of uniqueness," comments creative director Louis Gagnon.

The custom blends were derived by mixing existing PANTONE shades to create special new colors. These were printed in full strength to bleed across the outside and the inside of these bags, epitomizing the luxurious nature of the brand.

To reinforce the seductive nature of these bags, Paprika also used various high-quality finishing processes, including foil blocking, lamination, and the inclusion of matching-colored metal eyelets that hold in ribbon and cord handles neatly.

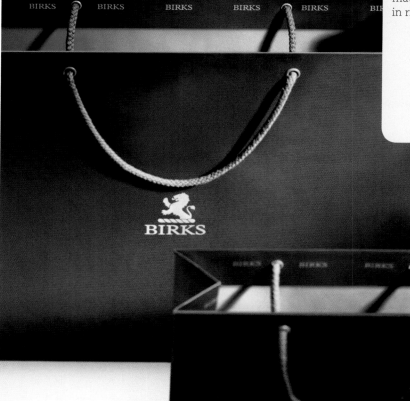

Fabric labels were woven in colors that match those chosen for print. It is interesting to view these labels from the rear as the type, although in reverse, still has surprisingly sharp detail, an effect which could also be utilized in a label design.

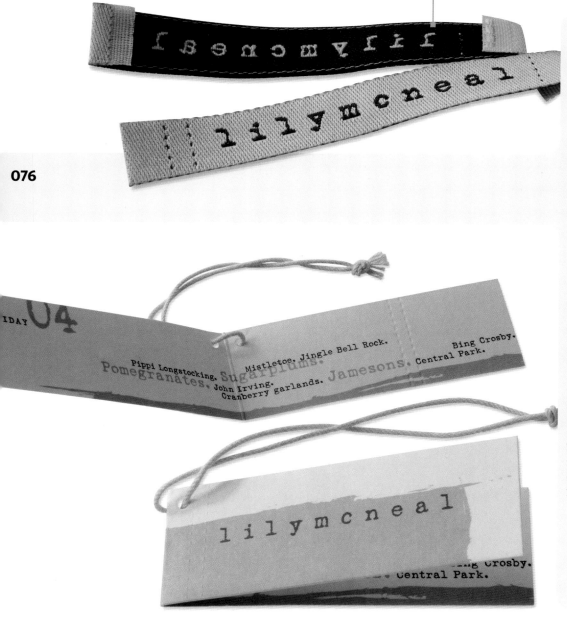

LILY MCNEAL

DESIGN
KBDA

SPECIFICATIONS
▌ Two-color lithography
▌ Scoring
▌ Perforation
▌ Woven fabric

These lily mcneal hangtags are printed in two PANTONE colors. What makes this design unusual is the fact that the light gray color is a special pastel PANTONE. PANTONE pastel shades give a light, flat, solid color, as opposed to being made up by a halftone screen. They are created by blending different percentages of certain PANTONE inks with varying amounts of extender to create a lightened tone of the original color combination.

These hangtags also use scoring and perforation to create a fold, plus textured detail that is reminiscent of actual stitching. Light gray has been purposefully selected and combined with a deep, rich, warm brown. This not only creates a subtle, natural effect that reinforces the softness of lily mcneal knitwear, but also echoes the need for gentle care of the garment.

LA MILITA

DESIGN
IDEAS FRESCAS

SPECIFICATIONS
▪ Four-color lithography
▪ Spot varnish

This witty label makes pleasing use of quirky illustration. The design is also notable for the carefully selected use of spot varnish to draw attention to the shine of the female character's honey-colored hair. Spot varnishing is ideal if small amounts of a design would benefit from a noticeable sheen. Overall, the addition of this crucial area of gloss tells the viewer that this product is special, that it is the result of a considerable amount of care and attention, as well as reinforcing the shiny, sweet nature of honey.

The circular elements within this design have areas of overlap, and, because the inks are transparent, extend the number of colors that can be seen in this poster at no extra cost.

JANUARY 30
WITH BUSDRIVER
GREAT AMERICAN
MUSIC HALL

DEERHOOF

DEERHOOF CONCERT

DESIGN
THE SMALL STAKES

SPECIFICATIONS
▌ Three-color screen printing

The Small Stakes specialize in the use of high-quality screen printing for concert posters, which—as was the case with this design for Deerhoof—are often used to create point-of-purchase attraction. This design has been screen-printed using three transparent colors—yellow, magenta, and cyan—with a dominant fourth color, black, being achieved by cleverly overprinting all three colors. The colors and motifs of this design have been used as a visual representation of the Deerhoof sound.

SPENDRUPS WINES

DESIGN
ZION GRAPHICS

SPECIFICATIONS
▪ Two-color lithography including one
  metallic color

The labeling for Nygårda is printed simply in two-color litho, however, one of the PANTONE colors is metallic. Both sets of labels utilize black plus the same special metallic color.

The level of sparkle and reflectivity produced by PANTONE metallic inks used in litho printing is generally not as great as what can be achieved with the use of foil blocking, but it is a much more cost-effective process. Different results can be achieved by careful selection of paper stock, and printing metallics onto coated paper or board produces some of the most metallic-looking results with this ink. However, selecting uncoated, absorbent material creates a very different, more subdued effect.

Varnishing areas printed with PANTONE metallic inks can also enhance the sparkle; this technique has been employed by Subplot Design Inc., as seen on pages 104–105.

LA MODE: BUY NOW – FOR SALE

DESIGN
ZION GRAPHICS

SPECIFICATIONS
▮ Two-color lithography

Advances in print capabilities have considerably expanded the creative possibilities available to graphic designers, and there is no doubt that technological breakthroughs have influenced the design decisions made by Zion Graphics for this La Mode LP labeling. Vinyl labeling is printed in two-color lithography using gray and black on white labeling. The colors, particularly the black, have been carefully selected to match the shade of the record exactly. At first sight, a viewer sees one individual, circular, gray label that appears to thread through from one side to the other. This is due to the precise positioning and control of the labeling shape and color.

Mode 002

La Mode

Buy Now
For Sale

Written, produced and
arranged by Steve Angello
& Sebastian Ingrosso.
Recorded at Oversized
Studios Stockholm for
La Mode 2005. Published
by Universal Publishing.
Manufactured by Euro Disc.
Distributed by Unique
Records and Distribution
UK. Made in Sweden.

The high-quality litho printing commissioned by Zion Graphics has enabled the ingenious incorporation of the very subtle effect created by the grooves of a record into the labeling design. This allows the style of design, combined with the selected method of printing, to create a highly contemporary piece that has an obvious affinity with the style of music.

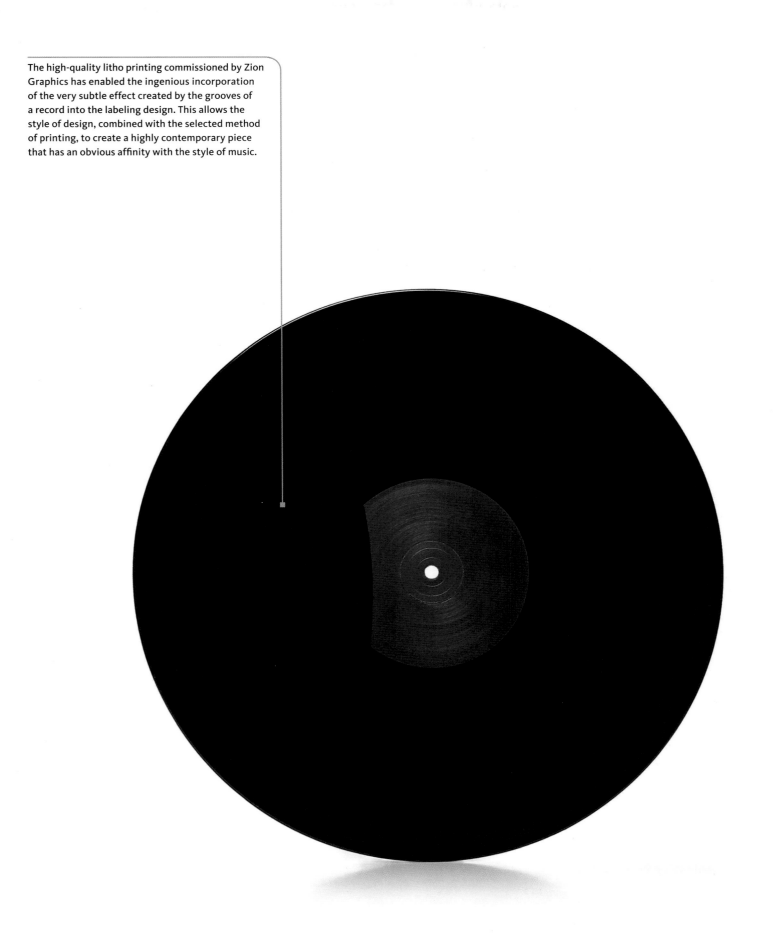

FLOOR UNIT POINT OF PURCHASE

CADBURY FLAKE DARK

DESIGN
V4 STUDIO/CADBURY TREBOR BASSETT

SPECIFICATIONS
▌"PMYK"
▌White screen printing
▌Metallic polyester 180 corrugate
▌Die-cutting

"PMYK" as opposed to CMYK inks were specified by V4 Studio for this point-of-purchase design. The "P" in this case stands for Cadbury's signature color purple, and is present in place of cyan ink. By specifying a precise, specially mixed purple, V4 could ensure absolute corporate color consistency throughout every chocolate brand within Cadbury's extensive portfolio.

Metallic polyester plays a fascinating role within the visual language of this design. "The metallic substrate was used to mimic the bar wrapper and also to give the unit a premium and indulgent feel," comments Carol Meachem of V4 Studio.

SWINGTAGS

SID

DESIGN
MORROW MCKENZIE DESIGN

SPECIFICATIONS
▮ Three-color lithography with custom-blended inks
▮ Fluorescent color
▮ Die-cutting
▮ Metal eyelets

These sid swingtags were printed
in custom-blended inks as well as a
fluorescent lime. Custom-blended inks
are created by mixing standard PANTONE
hues to create special one-off colors.
In this instance, the effect is heightened
because the colors are teamed with a
fluorescent lime, and complemented by
a carefully selected bright blue cord. The
color palette, combined with metal eyelets
and die-cutting, suggests a technological,
contemporary business with a focus on
the science of sport.

Artwork&design by vault49

SARULA

Sarula {sä'rōo-lä}   Black Widow Honey

Lower Lower Rise
Slimmer Flare Leg

vault49.com

SARULA

Sarula {sä'rōo-lä}
Black Widow Honey

LABEL

PROCESSED BLACK JEANS

DESIGN
VAULT49

SPECIFICATIONS
▪ Full-color lithography
▪ PANTONE special silver
▪ Spot varnish
▪ Die-cutting

A number of specialist print processes have been combined to create this elaborate label design for Processed Black Jeans. Vault49 added special PANTONE metallic silver and spot varnish to its four-color "print process recipe." This creates a surprising, subtle sheen and sparkle that tells the viewer that not only is the label a special design, with great attention to detail, but that the jeans themselves possess these remarkable qualities.

BAG

LEMON JELLY

DESIGN
AIRSIDE

SPECIFICATIONS
▌ Single-color flexography

Airside used a standard method of printing, flexography, to customize this small, bright yellow bag for the band Lemon Jelly. The piece was printed in single-color black, and the designers went out of their way to create an item that was "directly reminiscent of slightly 'tacky' children's party bags," explains Airside's Anne Brassier. The color of the bag was also carefully selected, reinforcing this concept and reassuring the recipient that they are bound to have a great time at a Lemon Jelly gig.

NIKE HUARACHE 2K5

DESIGN
PLAZM MEDIA, INC.

SPECIFICATIONS
▮ Four-color laser printing
▮ Vinyl

This point-of-purchase design for Nike's Huarache 2K5 involves the use of many different materials and processes, but is remarkable for its use of large-scale color laser prints. This type of printing can prove very cost-effective, as there are no setup costs, and large-scale prints are easy to generate to the designers' exact specification. Fade-resistant inks can be printed directly onto a great variety of materials, including fabric, plastic, and paper, making this an ideal way of producing graphics for retail environments, where, even in the short term, light might otherwise affect color quality.

For other elements of this design, Plazm has used adhesive vinyl lettering to affix graphics to glass and bespoke wooden plinths.

Print and production techniques have been cleverly selected and used to reflect and reinforce the high-tech, contemporary nature of the product, in a way that would not necessarily have been as simple had only more traditional print and production techniques been used.

HUARACHE
2K5

NIKE MADDIE PURPLE AND MADDIE PINK

DESIGN
VAULT49/CINCO

SPECIFICATIONS
▮ Four-color laser printing

These two point-of-purchase panels for Nike were produced using high-quality, large-scale laser prints on translucent film. This allows rear illumination to enliven and enrich the colorful effect of energetic imagery, while adding a slightly reflective pearlescent quality to skin tones. Other examples of large-scale laser prints can be seen on pages 058, 059, 086, and 087.

RED KNOT

DESIGN
**KENDALL ROSS BRAND DEVELOPMENT
AND DESIGN**

SPECIFICATIONS
▌ Two-color lithography
▌ Matte and gloss varnish
▌ Embossing

Kendall Ross has used a combination of specialist printing and finishing processes to achieve the design vision for luxury wine brand Red Knot.

"The unique, hand-drawn knot has been printed in a PANTONE red, which has been set against a background created from two passes of black ink, creating an extra-rich effect. Areas of gloss and matte varnish were applied to reinforce the luxurious nature of this product and, combined with embossing, result in a pleasing tactile quality," comments designer David Kendall.

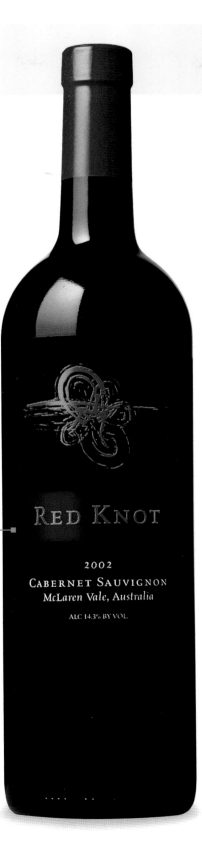

Two passes of the same PANTONE color can be used to enrich and intensify the final result, ensuring that the deepest, flattest shades have been achieved. In this instance, two passes of black have been used to give a truly opaque effect, which is reinforced by a coat of matte varnish.

ELIZABETH ARDEN SPA MATCH HAIRCARE

DESIGN
ALEXANDER ISLEY INC.

SPECIFICATIONS

■ Bags > offset printing, gloss varnish, die-cutting
■ Bottles > silk-screen printing, custom-mixed
   pearlescent colors

For this range of bags and labels the designers used specialist pearlescent inks. "The unusual shimmering properties of these colors were selected to reflect and reinforce the actual product effects and benefits," comments Lisa Scroggins of Alexander Isley.

The bags were printed in matching colors using offset litho. In order to create a similar surface shimmer and sheen, the design was gloss-varnished, and the finished print was die-cut and creased to form its final shape. A contrasting white cotton handle references the product color that features so prominently in the labeling.

The labeling on these bottles was directly screen-printed onto the surface, creating an ultra-smooth, pleasingly tactile result, reminiscent of the product's effect on skin. The containers are translucent, so the product itself plays an important role in the overall color palette of the labeling.

HUNT'S MUSTARD
AND KETCHUP

DESIGN
MATT GRAIF DESIGN

SPECIFICATIONS
▪ Four-color web offset printing
▪ Die-cutting

Hunt's Mustard and Ketchup labels were printed in four-color process, but rather than using conventional litho, they were printed on a web-fed press. Sheet-fed presses only allow for single-sided printing. Web-fed presses, however, are fed from a continuous roll of paper, making double-sided printing possible. Web printing is also far quicker than conventional litho presses, and tends to be used when large quantities of items are required.

Post-printing, these designs were die-cut to create the slightly curved shape for wrapping around bottles.

NURSERY SELECT

DESIGN
SOURCE INC.

SPECIFICATIONS
▪ Four-color flexography
▪ Shrink-wrap film

Source Inc. designed two sizes of packaging and labeling for Nursery Select, but it is the smaller shaker container labeling that forms the focus of this discussion. The ergonomically designed pack, with its soft, curving shape, fits very comfortably into the user's hand, but is a complex challenge for the labeling designer. Source's solution was to use flexography printing onto shrink-wrap film, thus allowing all of the smoothly curving, tactile container to be used to accommodate information.

Visually, this method of labeling has allowed Nursery Select to be positioned as a niche product for the more experienced gardener, telling potential purchasers that it is a unique product made from the highest-quality ingredients.

This shrink-wrap labeling was printed onto a shrink-wrap sleeve, with the artwork carefully constructed to accommodate the contours of the container. For the final shrinking process, the container is encased in the sleeve then passed through a "heat tunnel," causing the sleeve to shrink to fit, and the precisely configured labeling information to take on its intended final form and position.

MATERIALS

Bags, labels, and point-of-purchase items all have very practical functions. Bags are required to carry and protect purchases; labels inform potential buyers of the content, manufacturer, or designer, the size where necessary, and the price; point-of-purchase presentations give additional promotional information, establish a product's location, and often provide an appropriate container for display purposes. All of this could be done extremely simply, with plain paper bags (differing only in strength depending on the weight and character of the contents), plain paper labels with distinct black type, and equally unadorned, functional, point-of-purchase material.

"Too much decoration may be aesthetic noise, but decoration can also be the 'redundancy' that visual communication needs."

Redundancy, as the word suggests, is the part of design that could be omitted if mere function is to be satisfied, but in fact is vital if complex messages are to define one product from another in today's highly competitive markets. As Jonathan Baldwin and Lucienne Roberts remark, results may be decorative and elaborate, but instead of confusing readers, they actually enable fast transference of information.

Within the areas of bags, labels, and point of purchase, the creative and imaginative use of different materials is particularly valuable in constructing messages that communicate a wealth of information to readers. The weight, surface quality, unusual context, and unexpected combinations of materials all carry connotations that distinguish them and place them in categories that are generally recognized and understood. The general public is visually literate, and can usually read the intended messages instinctively.

In many respects, materials more than techniques belong to specific industries, parts of the world, periods of time, and codes of living, and as such have the power to carry a vast array of associations. For example, linen and hessian tend to connote natural, handmade influences, whereas metals and machined items connote masculinity or precision. Add to this the greater fluidity and flexibility of visual language compared with words, and communication to the widest possible audiences is achieved.

Communication is not a simple process of the designer creating a message that is received exactly as intended; receivers have their own experiences and expectations that influence their understanding. The strength of visual language constructed through the designers' use of different materials is the fact that readers are able to interpret the messages as they choose.

Materials also have a tactile quality that should not be underestimated in terms of producing successful bags, labels, and points of purchase. The sense of touch encourages an engagement with items, which often heightens the pleasure of the viewing process. It is evident that materials are often selected not only because of their visual qualities, but also for their tangible, tactile value.

This section of the book shows the use of many different materials in the contexts of bags, labels, and points of purchase, and although items may also include interesting print and production processes, the emphasis is on the use of particularly significant, unusual, or unexpected materials or combinations of materials.

WHITE STUFF

DESIGN
WHITE STUFF

SPECIFICATIONS
▪ Fabric labels > screen printing, stitching, cotton fabric, two types of ribbon, rough string
▪ Card labels > full-color lithography, duplexed board, rough string, mechanical distressing

White Stuff has designed a wide variety of unusual, complex labels based around fascinating combinations of materials and processes. Each label integrates a number of elements, discerningly selected from at least two types of ribbon, colorful screen-printed fabric, woven "White Stuff" nametape, and varied machine stitching, to create either a permanent sewn-in label or a temporary pinned-on hangtag.

A full-color card version utilizes a photographic interpretation of the elaborate fabric hangtag, printing an image of both sides of this stitched label onto red-cored duplex board. Rough brown string is incorporated into both types of tag, and the card is mechanically distressed on each corner to reveal its red core. Both the string and the distressing create stylish contrasts with the precision of the printing to form pleasing tags that reflect the style of White Stuff's vintage-inspired clothes.

Satin ribbon, natural string, ridged cream ribbon, silk-screened cotton fabric, and machine stitching synergize to reflect the highly individual combinations of materials and techniques that are the hallmark of White Stuff clothing.

APPLIED MATERIALS

DESIGN
GEE + CHUNG DESIGN

SPECIFICATIONS
- 6mm frosted plastic
- Cardboard
- Enamel-painted grommets
- 5mm black rubber
- Lithography
- Die-cutting

This incomparable carrier bag is made from frosted plastic. A very clever relationship between the printing and a die-cut cardboard insert provides a fascinating mixture of opaque and see-through areas. Four PMS colors (blue, copper, cream, and white) are printed on the inside of the plastic, and another two (blue and copper) on the cardboard insert. As Earl Gee of Gee + Chung Design says, "Applied Materials' innovation in silicon wafer manufacturing processes is reflected in the bag's unique materials and construction. A die-cut hole visually connects the company's 'Total Solutions' and 'Complete Systems' themes."

On this side of the bag, the cardboard inner is litho-printed in copper, with a circle cut through the center; the printing on the polyplast depicts a large lowercase "a" in solid dark blue as it overlaps the card, and a tint of the blue overprinting white, as it appears within the frosted circle. Together with the diagrammatic circles, the combination of different materials and processes creates an intriguing illusion it is not easy to differentiate between the elements of card, ink, and plastic.

This close-up shows the close match of the copper-enameled eyelets with the copper PMS, and the interesting black rubber handles. It also demonstrates the scope of the four-PMS lithography in reproducing solids, tints, and halftone images. The halftone images gain clarity through the strategic positioning of solid white or cream in the background.

BAG

NIKE BREAK FREE

DESIGN
PLAZM MEDIA INC.

SPECIFICATIONS
▌ Bag > velvet, machine stitching
▌ Label > two-color lithography, heavyweight board

Plazm designed a deep red velvet bag to contain a book promoting Nike's Break Free women's dance fitness line. The design of the bag, the book, and the swingtag was inspired by burlesque corsetry, hence the selection of luxurious, deep red velvet and contrasting shiny, delicate, black silk ribbon. The tag was printed in two-color litho and affixed by hand, helping to complete the viewer's impression of a special, overtly feminine, high-value product to remember.

WALES MILLENNIUM CENTRE

DESIGN
ELFEN

SPECIFICATIONS
- Bags > laser-cut vinyl arrows, readymade bags
- Tags > 750-micron board, single-color printing, white elastic bands

This carrier bag was produced to a very tight budget. Elfen's solution to applying design detail to the outside was to commission bright blue laser-cut vinyl arrows that are hand-applied to each bag. The arrows are adhered in a slightly different location each time, and even though the original bag is an off-the-shelf item, the overall effect is that of an unusual, highly individual designer piece.

Swingtags for the bags were printed in single color on heavyweight gray board. Continuing the theme of utilizing unusual material, Elfen has selected white elastic bands as ties for these tags. Uncommon materials and processes combined in a well-considered manner are a theme of this project, with both swingtag and bag creating an innovative, contemporary effect at no great expense.

The combination of material and processes gives the impression of a beautifully produced decorative piece, as the photo-etching has not only cut finely crafted, closely spaced small holes, but also engraved the details of a complex weather map into the satin-smooth surface of the tag.

HANGTAG

GIORGIO DAVANZO DESIGN

DESIGN
GIORGIO DAVANZO DESIGN

SPECIFICATIONS
▌ Photo-etching on aluminum

Giorgio Davanzo Design's self-promotional hangtag makes very unusual use of materials and processes: it is produced from a fine sheet of polished aluminum, with the design and information photo-etched into the surface. Lucky recipients are bound to be impressed by this highly crafted and precise keepsake, made from a different and unexpected material. Consequently, they are likely to attribute the quality of precise craftsmanship to its creators.

BAG

BIRDHEAD

DESIGN
PRANK DESIGN

SPECIFICATIONS
▮ Single-color screen printing
▮ Water-based inks
▮ Organic recycled cotton

Birdhead is an eco clothing company with a philosophy of "creating with less waste"; to this end, Prank Design was approached to produce a bag using only print and production processes that are in keeping with Birdhead's attitude to sustainability. This bag is made from organic recycled cotton, providing an ideal light-colored, slightly textured base for single-color silk-screen printing—using water-based inks, of course!

The clever theme of this bag is "Big Brother," and Prank has montaged a great number of images of eyes. Reproductions of the eye are well known as images that will attract attention, and this is exactly what is happening with this design.

JACKET

STROBE-LITE CYCLING COMMUTER JACKET

- 360° Strobe-Lite visible from 1/2 mile
- 200 hrs before changing batteries
- 3M™ Scotchlite™ Reflective Protection
- Lightweight Battery Casings
- Double-Taped Seams + Weatherproofing
- Superior Breathable Fabric

INSTRUCTIONS

BATTERY INSTALLATION
- Remove Clip
- Insert Batteries
- Snap on Cap

POWER OPERATION
- Push Once for ON
- Push Again for OFF

WASHING GARMENT
- Slide Lenses out of Clear Channels
- Wash Garment as per Instructions

The paper section involves a number of different-sized pages, with a cutting form used to create a clever curved clasp to hold them all in place. Subplot commissioned a die to cut the curved corners of the polypropylene.

HANGTAG

CYCLITE

DESIGN
SUBPLOT DESIGN INC.

SPECIFICATIONS
- Four-color lithography
- Fluorescent inks
- Spot-color silver
- Clear foil blocking
- Single-color screen printing
- Polypropylene
- Die-cutting

Subplot's design for this CycLite hangtag is a complex piece that makes prominent use of transparent polypropylene. This durable, flexible material was screen-printed in opaque white. When hanging in front of the paper-based part of the tag, it reveals the distinctive fluorescent green of the tag below. The layered effect of unusual materials, combined with the processes used, mimics the layers of technical fabric used to create CycLite clothing.

The paper-based section of the tag uses a fascinating mix of inks and print processes: four-color litho is complemented by the use of fluorescent green ink and spot-color silver, and clear foil blocking is used on the silver areas alone, in order to increase reflectivity.

BAG

ZOLOFOLIO

DESIGN
PALAZZOLO DESIGN

SPECIFICATIONS
▌ Cut and stitched carpet padding

Designers are constantly on the lookout for unusual materials that can enrich their work, enhance its individuality, ensure its memorability, and generally make their designs stand out from the crowd. Palazzolo Design sourced a unique material from the totally different context of carpeting. The company was looking to create a special case to hold client presentation samples which would say something about the distinctive personality of the Palazzolo brand.

The carpet padding has been cut and stitched along each edge to create an unusual, long-lasting container. The durability of this sturdy textile, along with the individuality of its recycled composition, ensures that each case will be kept longer than many of its paper-based alternatives.

RUCKLEY

DESIGN
RUCKLEY

SPECIFICATIONS
▪ Single-color printing
▪ Spot UV varnish
▪ Heavyweight stock

Ruckley carrier bags are made from a distinctive heavyweight board printed in single-color black prior to matte lamination and spot UV varnishing. The choice of board, and the addition of laminate, makes the bag uncommonly rigid and sturdy. These materials say that the bag is integral to the product, will not be disposed of lightly, and is an item of value in its own right. Add the subtle and sophisticated UV varnish that highlights the namestyle, plus the black rope handle, and there is no doubt that this bag and its contents will be perceived as high-quality and luxurious.

UV varnish, precisely registered over the namestyle, contrasts dramatically with the black matte surface of the bag. It is particularly effective because the rigidity of the card keeps the surface of the bag completely flat.

TUMI FLOW

DESIGN
MSLK

SPECIFICATIONS
- Paper tag > one-color offset printing, die-cutting
- Polypropylene tag > two-color metallic printing,
  die-cutting

MSLK designed a pair of hangtags to
complement bag maker Tumi's Flow range.
A less expensive paper tag was produced
to accommodate custom information for
each bag, while a more costly iridescent
polypropylene version is common to all.
The paper tag is printed in single color,
while its plastic partner uses two metallic
shades, each carefully selected to pick up
on the colors of zips and metal grommets.
Both labels were die-cut to reflect the
accent shaping and futuristic design
of the Flow range.

PUBLIK

DESIGN
SUBPLOT DESIGN INC.

SPECIFICATIONS
▮ Beer mats › four-color process, pulp board
▮ Menus › foam-lined high-gloss vinyl, debossing

Publik is a casual, energetic bar in Vancouver that encourages interaction. Subplot Design used a wide variety of contrasting materials to reinforce and express this mission within Publik's promotional material. Beer mats use four-color process on an open-textured, absorbent, wood-based pulp board, which is commonly used for beer mats and coasters because of its "blotting paper" qualities. It should be noted that when producing artwork for a material with this degree of absorbency, dot gain has to be carefully assessed.

Menus utilize an ultra-shiny vinyl covering that has been printed with one spot color, and double-printed with opaque white. Apart from the high-gloss surface, some of the advantages of this material are flexibility and durability. In this example, printed vinyl is heat-sealed over a foam backing, giving the cover an uncommon, pleasing, soft and squashy depth.

SENOK TEA

DESIGN
GIORGIO DAVANZO DESIGN

SPECIFICATIONS
- Single-color screen printing
- Aluminum sheet
- Clear satin finish

Three-dimensional point-of-purchase design can be crafted using many different materials; this display is fabricated out of 16-gauge aluminum, and is coated with a layer of clear anodized satin finish. The display was screen-printed in single color with brand information.

This image shows the structure of the design, highlighting cuts and folds that create precisely sized and located positioning for the products.

The use of this durable metallic material tells potential buyers that Senok produces a high-quality, fresh, contemporary, stylish drink.

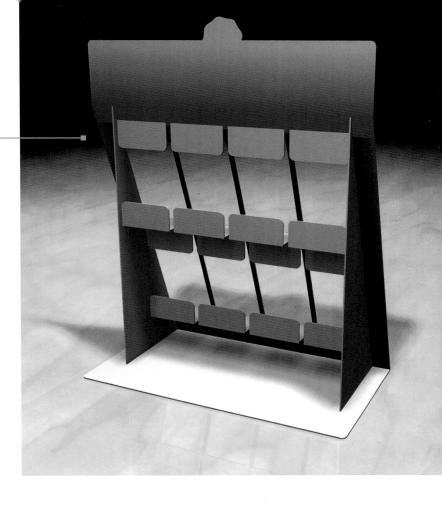

Senok's Gold and Silver tea labels are used to customize tea tins, and are each produced using two-color litho print on high-gloss crack-back label material. Each variety is printed in black, plus one PANTONE metallic color. This combination achieves a metallic quality not unlike that already seen on Senok's point of sale.

SILVER
LIMITED EDITION
LOOSE WHOLE-LEAF BLACK TEA

S
SENok

NET WEIGHT 1.75 oz (50 g)

GOLD
LIMITED EDITION
LOOSE WHOLE-LEAF BLACK TEA

S
SENok

NET WEIGHT 1.75 oz (50 g)

VITAM IMPENDERE VERO AND GRAJSKA ZAMETOVKA WINE

DESIGN
KROG, LJUBLJANA, SLOVENIA

SPECIFICATIONS
- Three-color lithography
- Foil blocking
- Laid paper

These two wine labels both use the same distinctive material and processes. The paper used is a textured, laid stock, with an effect that was originally created by the wire marks that ran through the papermaker's mold. When the paper was allowed to dry, these were transferred in subtle "watermark" mode to the finished sheet. This material, combined with the use of gold foil blocking, is evocative of traditional high quality—a message that is conveyed by association to the wine contained in both bottles. These labels are both printed in three PANTONE colors using lithography, with tints used to expand the color range within the designs.

PRANK

DESIGN
PRANK DESIGN

SPECIFICATIONS
▌ Static-shielding material
▌ Heat sealing

There is a great variety of attractive, fascinating materials available, many of which can be sourced from areas outside design. Prank Design regularly produces "fun packs" to use as promotional items, often using readymade bags of differing types. With Fun Pack 2, Prank used a bag made from static-shielding material, more commonly seen with computer grommetry. The plastic has an attractive, intriguing surface, in that it produces a silver sheen while being totally transparent. This allows the viewer to read information on the printed items within, thus saving Prank the expense of printing directly onto the static shield.

The bags are formed by heat-sealing the side edges to create a crisp, wide, flat seam on each side. Even after this process, the silvered sheen of the material is maintained. Visually, the use of this reflective material and finishing process gives the impression that the items contained within are special and, when released from the bag, will have a surprising, impactful effect. (Prank Fun Pack 1 can be seen on page 121; this also makes fascinating use of materials and processes.)

CROATIAN NATIONAL TOURIST BOARD

DESIGN
STUDIO INTERNATIONAL

SPECIFICATIONS
▪ Fabric bag > four-color flexography
▪ Cardboard bag > four-color lithography

Studio International designed a number of carrier bags to promote Croatia as a tourist destination. These two examples were both produced using unconventional materials to ensure durability and encourage repeat usage.

The fabric bag was printed using four-color flexography, and can be washed and used again and again. The cardboard bag, also printed in four color, but this time using lithography, is constructed in heavyweight card, creased and folded so as to form a box with an added rope handle. Both bags provide noticeable and practical platforms for displaying the Croatian Tourist Board's identity and message.

CROATIA
Croatian National Tourist Board

The Mediterranean as it once was

LABEL

CLUB 1984

DESIGN
PALAZZOLO DESIGN

SPECIFICATIONS
▪ Debossing
▪ Aluminum sheet
▪ Various fabrics

Using material more familiar within the realm of engineering, Palazzolo Design produced an unconventional label design for Club 1984. Details have been debossed into thin aluminum sheet and then stamped out to form leaf-shaped labels. The visual synergy of metallic labels against vibrantly colored animal-print fabric resembles the outlandish interior space of Club 1984, and reflects and accentuates the individuality of the clientele. The exceedingly durable, reflective, and tactile qualities of aluminum are not often found within the palette of raw materials used by the graphic designer. This means Palazzolo's label is likely to be talked about and preserved.

www.gourmetorganix.com

GOURMET ORGANIX

DESIGN
FORM

SPECIFICATIONS
▌ Flexography
▌ Biodegradable carrier bag

Some of the most fascinating developments in graphic materials have been involved with concern for sustainability and the environment. This bag, designed by Form for Gourmet Organix, is an excellent example. It uses completely biodegradable plastic to reinforce the organic theme. Using this innovative material provides designers with the reassuring knowledge that instead of contributing to landfill mountains and carbon emissions, their bag, after its useful life is complete, can have a much gentler impact upon the planet. The surface of the material is suitable for quality printing in any number of colors.

These 100% biodegradable carrier bags provide an environmental alternative to plastic or paper. They are made primarily from cornstarch which, in the right conditions, will biodegrade completely by returning to water, carbon dioxide, and compost. Some manufacturers of this type of bag state that, in the right conditions, their product will decompose within 45 days without leaving any harmful residues. The bags are as strong as conventional plastic bags, enabling them to be reused in a number of ways, including lining for small bins containing compostable waste, for which they provide the added advantage of biodegrading along with their contents.

WELLA COLOR PRESERVE SALON HAIRCARE

DESIGN
SHIMOKOCHI-REEVES

SPECIFICATIONS
- Five-color silk-screen printing
- Transparent adhesive labeling

The transparent properties of this adhesive labeling have been used to the full by Shimokochi-Reeves in its design for Wella Color Preserve by allowing the intense color of the container to remain in the background. White is printed first, in order to provide areas behind the colored symbols to ensure that they contrast clearly with the red container. The labeling's shiny, slightly silky surface suggests that customers' hair will gain the product's same sheen and quality.

LP BAG

LEMON JELLY

DESIGN
AIRSIDE

SPECIFICATIONS
▌ Red corduroy
▌ Machine stitching
▌ Hand embroidery

Corduroy is an uncommon material within graphic design, but Airside has selected this soft, ridged, tactile fabric to create a collectible 12in record bag for the band Lemon Jelly. The color of the corduroy was chosen to tie in with the bright red balloon that is a feature of the album cover. The bag was machine-stitched and the band's distinctive namestyle embroidered in contrasting yellow thread.

The image on the album cover is produced in a style reminiscent of British illustration of the 1920s and 1930s. It is perhaps for this reason that the long-time favorite fabric, corduroy, has been selected—albeit in a bright, contemporary color.

BATH HOUSE BATHING SUGARS

DESIGN
BATH HOUSE

SPECIFICATIONS
- Two- and four-color printing
- Ribbon
- Miniature clothespin

Very attractive and unusual use of materials within the labeling of these Bath House Bathing Sugars converts simple white-paper bags into desirable purchases. Two-color labels on the fronts of the bags pursue a fresh, traditional theme, while the combination of four-color labels, single-color labels, ribbons, and clothespins wrapping around the tops to secure the bags creates an extremely pretty and appealing presentation.

The back view of the top label and fastening mechanism on Shantung Silk reveals an amazing attention to detail: the red, orange, and gold silky ribbon feeds through a slit in the label, folds up and over the bag, and is held in place together with a single-color tag by a delightful little wooden clothespin. The synergy of such an interesting mix of materials, grouped with so much care and consideration, makes these products appear handmade and irresistible.

LABELS

3P ART. WORKS.

DESIGN
PALAZZOLO DESIGN

SPECIFICATIONS
■ Custom-formed plastic

In this example, Palazzolo commissioned the production of elaborate, miniature, adhesive picture frames to use as labels on slipcases for client 3P Art. Works. This range of unconventional labels was custom-formed in plastic, sprayed silver, and artificially aged to create a unique labeling device. This results in a number of levels of visual meaning—from value to individuality to collectibility—that impact on the contents of the slipcase. Custom-forming with plastic is an efficient way to create an intricately detailed three-dimensional label of this nature.

PRANK

DESIGN
PRANK DESIGN

SPECIFICATIONS
▌Transparent plastic bag
▌Two-color screen printing

When creating this first Fun Pack, Prank Design wanted to exploit the visual language of children's "goodie bags." To this end the company selected transparent plastic bags to hold a selection of brightly colored card and sticker-based promotional items, and sealed these with a foldover silk-screened label stapled into place. The transparent oil bag allows the recipient a tantalizing view of the "goodies" contained within. (Prank's Fun Pack 2, on page 113, also makes intriguing use of materials.)

MAILER BAG

UNIFORM: SAFE-T

DESIGN
FORM

SPECIFICATIONS
▌ Transparent plastic bag
▌ Heat sealing

Form produced a remarkable bag as
a mailer for Uniform's Safe-T range of
T-shirts. It is formed by heat sealing
strong, transparent, unprinted plastic,
with a narrow valve to allow for inflation.
As the plastic is totally see-through, much
of the information found on the contents
of the mailer can be seen from the outside,
thus negating the need for any printing
onto the plastic. Each mailer contains a
poster and a T-shirt. The only additional
labeling required is an adhesive address
label and stamp.

This unconventional approach to a bag associates
Uniform's Safe-T with the visual language of
health and safety information. Stacked in boxes,
their material and form is reminiscent of medical
containers. When alternative materials are used in
unexpected contexts, they not only function well,
but can also communicate with a wider audience
because they include an element of surprise.

PLAIN LAZY SWINGTAGS

DESIGN
PLAIN LAZY LTD.

SPECIFICATIONS
- Two-color printing
- Die-cutting
- 400gsm recycled board

For its swingtag designs, Plain Lazy selected ultra-heavyweight recycled board to help create a lasting impression and to reinforce the company's relaxed attitude to life and its commitment to the environment. Designs were printed in two sets of colors and die-cut to create large, durable versions of the Plain Lazy identity. Die-cut heavyweight board has a pleasing, sturdy quality. The edges take on a slightly rounded effect that is reminiscent of the tactile qualities found within pieces of a jigsaw puzzle, giving the tags a playful character.

SPOON PUBLISHING

DESIGN
ZION GRAPHICS

SPECIFICATIONS
▮ Plexiglas
▮ Laser-cutting
▮ Foil

Ricky Tillblad of Zion Graphics used
the intriguing transparent qualities of
Plexiglas to create a bright and impactful
point of purchase for Spoon. Two thick
pieces of the material are laminated;
a vivid bright yellow is applied to the
underside of the base, and the namestyle
is cut out of the top section.

The cut-out namestyle is backed with a fine layer
of shiny silver foil, which, due to its highly reflective
qualities, exaggerates the viewer's perception of
depth and edge detail in the letterforms.

TIMBUKTUU COFFEE BAR

DESIGN
SAYLES GRAPHIC DESIGN

SPECIFICATIONS
- Hand-folded corrugated brown board
- Two-color screen printing
- Die-cutting
- Fine natural jute rope

A combination of unusual materials helps to create and reinforce the sense that customers are entering an "eccentric oasis" by coming into the Timbuktuu coffee bar. The bags featured here have handles and closure devices formed from a contrasting mix of corrugated brown board and natural jute rope. These materials were chosen to support and strengthen the distinctive, eccentric theme that Sayles created for the store's relaunch. Characterful illustrations and text decorating the outside of these items were printed using two-color silk-screen printing. (Another example of Sayles' design for Timbuktuu is shown on page 178.)

MONTEZUMA'S

DESIGN
MONTEZUMA'S CHOCOLATES LTD.

SPECIFICATIONS
- Flexography
- Frosted plastic
- Brown paper
- Cellophane

Montezuma's produces a diverse range of bags made from interesting and contrasting materials, including frosted plastic, brown paper, and cellophane. The range of bags covers every eventuality and marketing opportunity: frosted plastic bags give customers a tantalizing glimpse of Montezuma's products while also ensuring company branding is paramount; single-color blue is used across all these different surfaces; the visual language of the brown-paper bags emphasizes the handmade, organic nature of the chocolate; and the small cellophane bag, subtly printed with the company's Aztec illustration, ensures that customers making even the smallest purchase will have a branded memento.

LEMON JELLY

DESIGN
AIRSIDE

SPECIFICATIONS
▪ Embroidery
▪ Denim
▪ Screen printing
▪ Hessian

Lemon Jelly asked Airside to produce limited-edition bags for their 7in vinyl records, *Soft Rock* and *Rolled Oats*. The *Soft Rock* bag is made from dark blue denim and is brightly embroidered in a style used on denim clothes of the 1970s. The *Rolled Oats* bag is made from naturally colored hessian and screen-printed in two colors, again using a style that was popular in the 1970s.

The visual language of these two designs conveys meanings that are particularly appealing to a youth market with a fondness for 1970s retro. Designs, materials, and processes tell the viewer that Lemon Jelly's music is individual and quirky, and that those who buy these bags have a similarly "quirky" attitude to life. (Another Airside-designed Lemon Jelly bag is shown on page 118.)

PREŠERNOVO AND POZVAČIN WINE

DESIGN
KROG, LJUBLJANA, SLOVENIA

SPECIFICATIONS
▋ Four-color lithography
▋ Gold foil blocking

These wine labels make use of "branded" laid stock. For the Prešernovo wine, the designer chose to have the grain of the paper, and therefore the watermarking, running vertically down the label, thus accentuating the height of the bottle.

The labels are printed in four-color litho, highlighted with carefully positioned gold foil blocking. This finishing process, combined with the use of specialist paper, creates a sense of exclusivity and high quality as well as long-standing repute. (Another example of wine labeling by KROG is shown on page 112.)

BRIGHT PINK

DESIGN
BRIGHT PINK COMMUNICATIONS DESIGN

SPECIFICATIONS
▌ Ginger cookies
▌ Handwriting in icing
▌ Raffia

Christmas is a time of feasting and traditional foods, so what better "material" for self-promotional nametags than a spicy ginger cookie? By rolling out the mixture thicker than usual, and baking it in a cooler oven for a little longer, the biscuits become hard and durable. The heart symbolizes love to be shared at Christmas, the icing is a decorative element often identified with this time of year, and the raffia acts as a harmonizing element in the design through its color and natural character.

BATH HOUSE NATURAL SPA RANGE

DESIGN
BATH HOUSE

SPECIFICATIONS
▪ Single- and two-color lithography
▪ Textured paper
▪ String
▪ Fabric

By introducing a variety of materials into the range of labels and hangtags for its Natural Spa products, Bath House has been able to print in just two colors—brown and black—to realize extremely stylish, quality packaging that, as the manufacturer suggests, "reflects the wild beauty of the British countryside." On the bottles, very simple circular and rectangular labels are visually enhanced as they integrate with natural string; around the sack of Bath Salts, a single-color round white label is attached to, and complements, a band of light brown, heavyweight, textured paper.

A single-color label for White Meadow soap is held in place by a waxy translucent paper. This not only wraps around the label and the soap, but also creates a visually "misty" effect. A piece of string is tied in a knot on top to complete the traditional styling.

The visual impact of the labeling on this Wild Jasmine soap is established through a layering process, with different materials and textures interacting with each other. Translucent paper is partially covered by a label in the form of a band of textured white paper, which is overlaid with a band of linen. Circular self-adhesive sticker tops the design. From a purchaser's point of view, the amount of effort and attention to detail signifies that this is a very special handmade product.

A single-sided, single-color image of cornflowers is held inside a narrower, folded tag, and tied with rustic string to the Spa Bath Salts bag. All layers of the hangtag are printed on textured white card and, together with the attached wooden scoop, enhance the classic country style of this item.

bath house

Spa Bath Salts

White Meadow

An essential ingredient for the perfect bathing ritual.

Add a spoonful of these finely ground bath salts to soften and gently fragrance bath water. Harmonize your mind, soul and spirit, gently cleanse your body, relax and enjoy some 'me' time.

White Meadow

bath house

wild jasmine

CADBURY CREME EGG

DESIGN
V4 STUDIO / CADBURY TREBOR BASSETT

SPECIFICATIONS
▌ "PMYK" screen printing
▌ Display board
▌ Pre-colored Foamex
▌ Clear polypropylene
▌ Plastic rivets

A considerable mix of materials was selected by V4 Studio for the production of its semipermanent point-of-purchase design for Cadbury's Creme Egg. "We chose Foamex, used for the base of this unit, for its durability," says Carol Meachem of V4 Studio. She continues, "We used pre-colored polypropylene and display board to give the design a premium quality feel, and also because both of these substrates are recyclable."

This design uses "PMYK" screen print, the cyan ink being replaced with Cadbury's special purple. Where practical, Cadbury regularly substitutes purple for cyan in a four-color process.

WUNDERBURG DESIGN

DESIGN
WUNDERBURG DESIGN

SPECIFICATIONS
▌ Smoked sealing wax
▌ Personal seal

"Using carefully selected materials to create harmony and interest is an important component in our corporate design," says Annette Ruland of Wunderburg Design. With this philosophy in mind, Wunderburg seals its gray DL envelopes with smoked gray sealing wax, imprinting it with the company's personal stamp to form a striking and unusual three-dimensional "sticker." This clever use of traditional material in a contemporary color, and on a stylish envelope, immediately communicates to recipients Wunderburg's unique thinking and design expertise.

LIVE ARTS

DESIGN
BOING!

SPECIFICATIONS
- Single-color lithography
- Readymade fluorescent star stickers
- Rubber-stamping

Readymade items of stationery can provide useful, visually exciting, and cost-effective ways of augmenting, or indeed styling, low-budget projects. The brochure cover for Live Arts uses readymade, fluorescent star-shaped stickers, printed in single-color, to inject an area of otherwise unaffordable liveliness and brightness. The stickers were applied by hand at the end of the brochures' production, placed precisely in the gap provided by the rubber-stamping used to create the title. This hand-finishing process adds a pleasing tactile quality to the brochure.

ETC

DESIGN
BRIGHT PINK COMMUNICATIONS DESIGN

SPECIFICATIONS
■ Single- and four-color lithography
■ Die-cutting
■ Cotton binding
■ Stitching

This range of swingtags for accessories brand etc was produced in both four-color and single-color print, and each tag has been die-cut to create an oversize hole that accommodates the tie. This cut-out is also an integral part of the design, and speaks to any potential purchaser of etc products' unconventional, contemporary approach to design. The tag uses both paper and fabric. Each tag has a bound edge that is covered with black cotton binding, and the mix of materials reflects and reinforces the unusual nature and design detailing of etc products.

WHITE STUFF

DESIGN
WHITE STUFF

SPECIFICATIONS
- Four-color lithography
- Matte art paper
- Foil-lined envelopes

"Grow your own 'sweet white'," say the packets of Alyssum that were distributed at the point of purchase for White Stuff clothing. To reference the brightness and vitality of White Stuff clothing, displays of potted flowers, gardening implements, and packets of seeds accompany the in-store mannequins. "Spread some hugs, kisses, cuddles, and smiles," the seed packets suggest.

This point-of-purchase concept relies on careful presentation and hard processes, turning seed packets into hangtags, and integrating the gardening theme.

138

RIGGS&FORSYTHE

DESIGN
PEAR DESIGN

SPECIFICATIONS
- Clear plastic pressure-sensitive labels
- Four-color screen printing with two passes of white

The bottles in this range have a very tactile quality, with columns of vertical ribs debossed into the surface and the R&F logo embossed on the front. Clear plastic pressure-sensitive labels contribute to the overall effect by merging with the bottle, and complementing the ridged texture with their, soft, smooth character. They are screen-printed in four colors, with two passes of white to give the graphics sharper detail. The design upholds Riggs&Forsythe's upmarket image.

139

FINISHING

Die-cutting, embossing, debossing, foil blocking, and engraving all fall into this section. These processes epitomize an attention to detail that individualizes bags, hangtags, and point-of-purchase items, stamping distinctive visual characteristics on designs to make them unusual and memorable.

One of the most popular finishes is die-cutting, when cut edges or cut-out shapes cannot be handled by a straight-edged guillotine, and a cutting form is created in order to give designs such features as curves, holes, pockets, and fastening devices. Within point of purchase, the use of a cutting form can be comparatively functional, in terms of producing a flat net that is then creased and folded to form a display container. However, most of the examples in this section show how cutting forms have customized the shapes of tags, labels, and cut-out handles on bags so that they become an integral part of a product's identity. Shape and form are as important as color, choice of typeface, image content, and composition when determining a visual identity. The Moving Picture Company carrier bags by Form demonstrate this, as their bag handle is a punched-out rectangle with concave sides—a shape derived from the company logo (see page 177).

Embossing and debossing require a specially created stamp to raise or recess an area into a printed or unprinted section of the paper. These purely decorative processes tend to imply exclusivity and quality in a product.

Many of the finishes in this section, including foil blocking and engraving, are selected by designers purely for their aesthetic characteristics, which carry meaning in terms of identity and style. Foil blocking, for example, whether it is produced in glossy metallic or solid rich color, creates a crisp, slightly indented, tactile surface that is distinctive and recognizable as a sign of quality. Gunther Kress and Theo van Leeuwen talk of the value of the interrelationship of material, surface, and process in communicating meaning:

"Inscription comprises the interrelated semiotic resources of surface, substance, and tools of inscription. Each has its own semiotic effects, and in their interaction they produce complex effects of meaning."

Finishing processes are consistently labor-intensive, with special tools needed to cut, block, engrave, stitch, or crease designs to create specific effects. In appreciating the results, viewers are in a sense aware of the procedures required to achieve them, and enjoy not only what they see, but also what they experience: threading a finger through an interestingly shaped hole or caressing a raised or shiny surface. Although many of the examples in this section beg to be handled, merely observing them can provide a worthwhile manner of imbibing design detail.

BAGS, HANGTAG, AND BUSINESS CARD

PEARL

DESIGN
IE DESIGN + COMMUNICATIONS

SPECIFICATIONS
- Two-color lithography
- Die-cutting
- Embossing

Two PMS colors were printed independently, and overprinting each other in order to give the effect of three colors within the decorative namestyle of "Pearl." One of the PMS colors is also printed in an all-over complementary pattern on the inside of the hangtag. Pearlescent stock was selected to highlight the name of the store, a cutting form was used to create the distinctive shape of the business card, and the circle in the swash of the "R" was embossed.

BANKERWESSEL

DESIGN
BANKERWESSEL

SPECIFICATIONS
∎ Single-color flexography
∎ Die-cutting

Bankerwessel's adhesive single-color label has a distinctive elephant shape. This delightful little character, with the company's web address running around one ear, is printed on transparent label stock die-cut into an elephant shape, so that whatever the color behind the sticker, the red elephant appears to be sitting directly on it.

BAG

THE BELLEVUE COLLECTION FASHION WEEK'06

DESIGN
**KENDALL ROSS BRAND DEVELOPMENT
AND DESIGN**

SPECIFICATIONS
▮ Four-color lithography
▮ Coated stock
▮ Ribbon handles

The Bellevue Collection swag bag was printed in full color onto luxurious matte-coated stock, to be given out to attendees at Bellevue shows. A distinctive feature of the design is the specialist silk-ribbon handles. These were applied to add a sense of glamor not only to the bag itself, but also to the individual who is carrying it.

THE GETTY CONSERVATION INSTITUTE

DESIGN
KBDA

SPECIFICATIONS
▮ Four PANTONE colorways
▮ Screen printing
▮ Die-cutting
▮ Scoring
▮ Folding

The Getty Conservation Institute shopping bags were screen-printed on high-quality cover paper, in the four different colorways, each using two special PANTONE colors. The bags were die-cut, scored, and folded, with two holes that, once the bag is filled and the handles put together, align precisely to accommodate a strong tie. Bringing the reinforced handles together in this manner gives the bag extra strength to cope with weighty items.

ETC

DESIGN
BRIGHT PINK COMMUNICATION DESIGN

SPECIFICATIONS
- Four-color laser printing
- Die-cutting
- Hand-folding

Designed to label etc products' more prestigious and traditionally inspired creations, these swingtags were laser-printed in a variety of colorways, die-cut, then carefully assembled. As with many elaborate tag designs, the tag has become as much a part of the highly desirable purchase as the actual product. In the case of these miniature dolls, the wide variety of colors, combined with the hand-finishing, ensures that every doll is a unique, one-off piece that adds considerable value to the purchase.

XTZ INDUSTRIES
TURBO TRUFFLE

DESIGN
TRAIN OF THOUGHT

SPECIFICATIONS
▪ Four-color process
▪ Varnish
▪ Die-cutting

The Turbo Truffle Blender allows a customer to select his or her own preferred chocolate caffeine "hit." This point-of-purchase container provides easy access to the range of chocolates contained within. It has been produced by printing in full color onto durable heavyweight board, followed by varnishing. The surface design uses the same colors as used to wrap the individual flavors of the truffles themselves, with colors exactly matching those printed on the plastic wrappers.

The design has been die-cut to create the innovative angled drawer that provides easy access to the product. Using cardboard for the Turbo Truffle Blender means that once one point-of-purchase unit is empty, it can be recycled and replaced with a new, completely full unit.

HONEY B

DESIGN
LAURA VARSKY

SPECIFICATIONS
▌Marker pen

Laura Varsky was commissioned by Gary Lo to help promote his range of toys. The resulting point-of-purchase designs were produced by hand, using nothing more complicated than a few marker pens. Working directly onto the plastic "creatures," Laura selected gold and black permanent marker pens to ensure durability of design. This method of production provides the opportunity for a great deal of design flexibility, and also means that each finished character is totally individual.

148

ELENI'S NEW YORK CONVERSATION COOKIES

DESIGN
STORMHOUSE PARTNERS

SPECIFICATIONS
- Four-color lithography
- Spot varnish
- Foil blocking
- Color laser printing

150

These labels have metallic foil blocking around their perimeter, and were designed so that the labels on the back can be laser-printed to order. They are supplied to the shop as blanks, with just the silver border printed, together with a number of full-color designs that can be printed within the labels on an ink-jet or laser printer, as demand dictates.

The concept is extremely practical and effective; the quality and professional character of the silver reflects the high-end positioning of the product. The cookies carry personal and individual messages, and producing the labels only when they are required saves the client from deciding how many of each to order. The client requested gingham as part of the pack style in order to evoke traditional home baking, and its linear structure has made the positioning of the rear labels by the client comparatively easy.

TASTE OF BRANSON

DESIGN
MATT GRAIF DESIGN

SPECIFICATIONS
▮ Offset lithography
▮ Four-color process
▮ Die-cut ribbon
▮ Hand gluing

The finishing processes used for these labels involve die-cutting color-co-ordinated ribbon and hand-gluing this material to seal the lids. Each label design for this range makes distinctive use of gingham (reminiscent of traditional-style tablecloths and kitchens) and also of a bright blue, printed vertical ribbon, again reminiscent of country fair prizes. These themes are carried through to the hygiene seal of the lid.

BAG

PALAZZOLO STAMPS

DESIGN
PALAZZOLO DESIGN

SPECIFICATIONS
▪ Four-color lithography
▪ Gummed stock with pinwheel perforation

Distinctive pinwheel perforation has been used to separate individual stamp designs. A considerable variety of individual stamps have been printed in full color on sheets of old-fashioned gummed stock.

This bespoke, hand-worked perforation has helped to create an interesting tactile quality, a sense of individuality from a bygone era, and, most importantly, ensured the easy separation of each stamp.

Palazzolo Design applied these perforated stamps to the outside of their company's metal portfolio. The portfolio itself uses an unusual finishing process—natural acid etching—to give it a deliberately aged, "period" feel.

BIANCA WASH JEAN

DESIGN
VAULT49

SPECIFICATIONS
- Full-color lithography
- One PANTONE special color
- Embossing
- Die-cutting

Vault49's design for the Bianca Wash Jean label has a complex list of print and production specifications, and the two finishing processes are especially effective. This label was printed in CMYK plus one special PANTONE color, then finished with embossed detail, adding a tactile dimension to the already highly ornamental design. This elaborate label, aimed at a youthful female market, helps to communicate information concerning the detailed design of Bianca Wash Jeans.

SARULA
Sarula {sä'rōō-lä}
Black Widow Honey

Artwork&design by vault49

SARULA
Sarula {sä'rōō-lä}   Black Widow Honey

Lower Lower Rise
Slimmer Flare Leg

vault49.com

SCHUH SPRING/ SUMMER 2005

DESIGN
STUDIO OUTPUT

SPECIFICATIONS
▌Four-color process
▌Die-cutting

Studio Output designed four-color point-of-purchase material for footwear company Schuh. Shoe designs that evoke the styles of the 1970s and appeal to a fashion-conscious youth market are portrayed within four-color posters and three-dimensional display pieces. Die-cutting was used to achieve effective three-dimensional constructions, and to produce simple cut-out shapes to apply to their fronts. The applied shapes literally provide each item with "stand-out" quality that gives maximum visibility and impact. The display stands are self-supporting, and therefore do not require fixing to any surfaces.

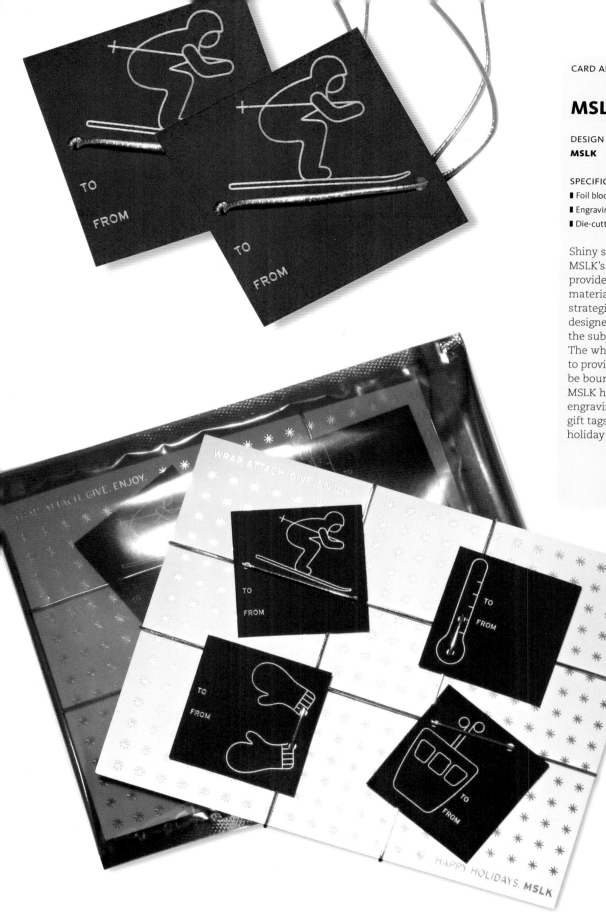

CARD AND GIFT TAG

MSLK 2006

DESIGN
MSLK

SPECIFICATIONS
▪ Foil blocking
▪ Engraving
▪ Die-cutting

Shiny silver elastic cords, selected for MSLK's 2006 holiday gift tag designs, provided the inspiration for all other materials and processes used. The tags' strategically positioned die-cut holes are designed to interact purposefully with the subject matter of each illustration. The white holiday cards are duplexed to provide extra rigidity, enabling them to be bound by the elastic of the gift tags. MSLK have used silver foil blocking and engraving on the white cards and red gift tags to reinforce a shimmering, holiday feel.

The uncoated, soft, absorbent red stock contrasts with the shiny silver thread, foil blocking, and engraving, to give an exciting complementary combination of surface qualities that are intriguing to the touch. The attention to detail in the choice of materials and finishing processes creates an upmarket and sophisticated effect, despite printing with only two colors.

THERESA KATHRYN

DESIGN
IE DESIGN + COMMUNICATIONS

SPECIFICATIONS
▊ Two-color lithography
▊ Lamination
▊ Die-cutting
▊ Saddle stitching

158

"We wanted to bring the story of Theresa Kathryn, the person, to life by telling her inspiring story in the hangtag," says Kenny Goldstein of IE Design + Communications. This hangtag is indeed a beautifully crafted miniature book. The cover is litho-printed onto a heavyweight card, in pale blue on the outside and orange on the inside, matte-laminated on both sides, intricately die-cut, creased and folded asymmetrically, saddle-stitched, and clasped with a die-cut flap. On releasing the closure, eight pages of two-color text on matte-laminated white stock are revealed to complete this exquisite hangtag. This not only extols in words the smart, successful character of Theresa Kathryn products, but also demonstrates it through the pure quality and sophistication of the tag.

LABELS

VISAO BINOCULAR

DESIGN
MATT GRAIF DESIGN

SPECIFICATIONS
▌ Four-color process
▌ One special PANTONE (black)
▌ Foil blocking
▌ Holographics

These unusual V-shaped labels use a variety of processes, including four-color lithography, plus one extra PANTONE black. However, it is the two finishing processes that really give this design its prestige. First, gold foil blocking is used to highlight the Visao namestyle and to frame the edge of the label. The second, most uncommon, finishing process is the use of a holographic image of an eagle. This forms the center-piece of the design, and suggests the high quality and clarity of Visao binoculars.

A|X ARMANI EXCHANGE

DESIGN
ALEXANDER ISLEY INC.

SPECIFICATIONS
▮ Bags > offset lithography, machine stitching, custom-milled recycled paper
▮ Style selector > die-cutting, offset lithography

Alexander Isley Inc. has produced a wide range of bags, labels, and point-of-purchase items for A|X Armani Exchange. As would be expected for such a high-profile fashion company, bespoke materials and finishing processes were used to reinforce the potential purchaser's impression that Armani Exchange designs and produces high-quality, stylish clothing from premium materials, and with great attention to detail.

In the selection featured on these pages, a number of bags or boxes with handles are shown. The largest carrier bag is made from custom-milled recycled paper, and is printed in single-color offset litho. It is equipped with "clothes-line" handles, while the base is machine-stitched in the same manner as fertilizer bags. Boxes also feature washing-line handles, this time with smaller loops, which can also help to slide the drawer from the outer part of this container. A regular grid pattern of small circular holes has been die-cut across the front-facing surface of each box.

A point-of-purchase "style selector" has been designed to stand on countertops and, at a single glance, explain design and fabric combinations to the customer. This point-of-purchase item has been printed in single-color litho, and has a number of circular die-cuts punched through so that fabric samples can be easily displayed, and if necessary, touched by any potential purchaser.

Shirts and socks sport matching wraparound labels, which are printed in single color on the Armani custom-milled stock. Fabric labels are stitched onto jeans and shirts; although they are printed on a different material, they again match the color scheme of all other Alexander Isley-designed items.

FULLY LOADED

DESIGN
SUBPLOT DESIGN INC.

SPECIFICATIONS
- Tea boxes > five-color lithography, sealing varnish, die-cutting
- Display > bent, frosted Plexiglas, single-color screen printing
- Flavor menu > clear plastic frame

Subplot Design Inc. used a number of interesting finishing processes to create point-of-purchase material for fully loaded tea. Boxes containing individual flavors were printed in five-color litho and finished with die-cutting to create the unique drop-down drawer for restaurant and café display purposes. This bespoke method of presentation is an attractive alternative to the familiar ripped box front.

Individual tea boxes are grouped in sixes for display within a specially created Plexiglas point-of-purchase container. The Plexiglas has been cut, screen-printed, and specially heated along fold lines to allow for the formation of folds.

Die-cutting has allowed for the creation of this clever hinged opening. The drawer can be tilted open for easy access to teabags within, and also has a fascinating built-in "stop," meaning that the drawer cannot be opened too far. Cutting forms enable the production of a variety of intricate cut-out shapes and mechanisms, which can be economically reused for different colorways, and for subsequent reprints.

Naked Strawberry Green Tea

"Sameness" sucks. Call us a chic boutique hotel in a world of big, generic all-inclusive resorts. Our *Naked Strawberry Green Tea* can be found far off the beaten path, swingin' it with the locals. Vive la différence!

WHOLE LEAF GREEN TEA
with Strawberry Pieces and Rose Petals

fullyloadedtea™

14 PYRAMID BAGS
Premium Whole Leaf Tea
Thé supérieur feuilles entières
1.1 oz | 32.2 g

HARRY AND DAVID

DESIGN
MORROW MCKENZIE DESIGN

SPECIFICATIONS
- Two-color lithography
- Die-cutting

Simple two-color litho and carefully considered die-cutting have been used by Morrow McKenzie Design to achieve an Art Deco–inspired range of labels and tags for Harry and David dipping oil and olives. Each variety of bottled oil utilizes two adhesive labels: a small circular one is used to hygienically seal the lid, while a long, ribbon-shaped label extends to the full height of each bottle. Selecting to die-cut in this shape tells potential purchasers that this is a quality product, one that is possibly even prize-winning, and therefore of great value and rarity.

The ribbon-inspired theme has been carried through to the die-cut design of tags for Harry and David's Authentic Greek Olives, which are folded into four pages and tied with old-fashioned cotton string around the neck of the jars. Tags are also cleverly used to secure paper covers over the lids of these jars, providing Morrow McKenzie with a great opportunity for adding branding and product detail.

LABEL AND BAG

VRANAC WINE

DESIGN
KROG, LJUBLJANA

SPECIFICATIONS
▮ Three-color lithography
▮ Foil blocking
▮ Die-cutting

This KROG, Ljubljana project makes use
of two interesting finishing processes:
foil blocking and die-cutting. Labels, placed
within the upper third of a tall, slim bottle,
are litho-printed in three colors, and then
foil-blocked in gold. The combination of
finishing process, the shape and size of the
bottle, and the careful placing of the label
all help to position this product firmly
within a specialist, luxury section of the
wine market.

    Die-cutting was used to create a
bespoke carrier bag that was carefully
designed to accommodate the slim shape
of the bottle. The elongated form of this
bag is unusual and attracts attention
through its uncommon proportions alone;
the completely circular cut-out handle
emphasizes the exclusivity of this product.

BATH HOUSE
PAISLEY ROSE

DESIGN
BATH HOUSE

SPECIFICATIONS
▪ Two- and four-color lithography
▪ Textured paper
▪ Ribbon
▪ Braid

The tags for these two products utilize an appealing interplay between a number of different materials and the complex manner in which they are brought together at the finishing stage. Ribbon, braid, coated and uncoated papers, and textured and smooth papers combine within single tags, folded tags, self-adhesive labels, and a wraparound label (all using the same color palette) to form a cohesive and distinctive style.

The floral paisley pattern of this wraparound label is printed on uncoated, textured stock, and is complemented by a blue-and-white polka-dot hangtag on another uncoated, textured stock. The effect is completed by a perfectly matching blue silky ribbon, neatly knotted to hold the hangtag in place. Such detailed hand-finishing reflects on the products themselves and suggests they are to be used for self-indulgence.

PAISLEY ROSE

Bath Salts
PAISLEY ROSE

Add one or two spoons full of bath salts to warm running water for a sophisticated bath-time treat.

bath house

The Bath House, Sedbergh, Cumbria, LA10 5HF
www.thebathhouseshop.co.uk
tel 015396 21992 fax 015396 21912
Made in the UK.
Keep out of reach of children.

1kg e 35.1oz

CAFÉS EL MAGNÍFICO

DESIGN
SONSOLES LLORENS DISSENY GRAFIC

SPECIFICATIONS
▪ Tin labels > single-color offset lithography
▪ Box label > foil blocking
▪ Bags > single-color lithography

Foil blocking in copper was used to create the rectangular label that seals this pack of four coffees from Cafés El Magnífico. This finishing process was used to give the impression of exclusivity, luxury, and quality. The positioning of the label also draws attention to the brand. The labels for the coffee tins are printed in single-color litho, utilizing halftone background imagery to create a variety of shades from just one color. The same printing method was used for the carrier bags—a good example of the design possibilities that are achievable with halftone imagery.

EL PALACIO DE HIERRO

DESIGN
ALEXANDER ISLEY INC.

SPECIFICATIONS
- Offset printing
- Gloss and matte varnish
- Embossing

Designed to reflect the long-established, high-quality luxury shopping experience that can be found at El Palacio de Hierro, these bags and boxes were constructed in heavyweight board, with each featuring a sturdy, twisted rope handle. A distinctive and highly noticeable color combination gives each piece from this range a bright yellow front face, framed by a black edge. Yellow areas are matte-varnished, while all black elements, including the El Palacio de Hierro namestyle, are coated with a contrasting gloss varnish. Embossing is used precisely to raise the glossy black namestyle from the expanse of matte yellow.

BATH HOUSE
A NEW BABY

DESIGN
BATH HOUSE

SPECIFICATIONS
▋ Four-color lithography
▋ Silver foil blocking
▋ Uncoated stock
▋ Ribbon

Labeling for the A New Baby range from Bath House employs complementary fresh colors out of the four-color set, high-gloss silver foil blocking, and a matte surface of white uncoated stock. It also demonstrates a superb quality of silver foil blocking as an integral part of the design.

The label on the lid of A New Baby soap and sponge is an unusual cross between a hangtag, with white-and-green stripy ribbon threaded through a hole at the top edge, and an adhesive label. It looks like a hangtag, but is affixed to the box with two sticky pads that raise it slightly above the surface. Interesting and well-designed hangtags generally denote style, and the effect of this concept is to suggest that this is a "designer" product.

The silver foil blocking on this hangtag highlights the pleasing contrast of gloss and matte surfaces, and exemplifies the ability of the process to reproduce fine and very tiny lettering.

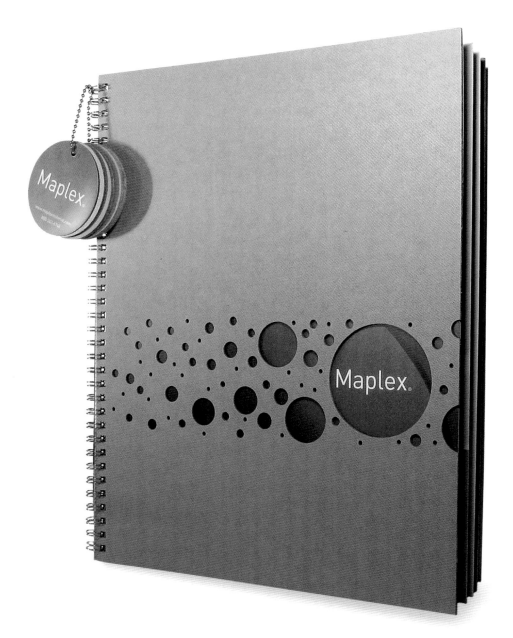

MAPLEX SWATCH

DESIGN
MSLK

SPECIFICATIONS
- Four-color process using vegetable-based inks
- Die-cutting

Maplex is an environmentally conscious company, and therefore wanted to find a way of getting its product samples into the hands of architects and designers in a sustainable manner. To accomplish this, MSLK designed a swatch in the form of a swingtag that cleverly uses the materials left over from die-cutting the brochure cover. It is attached to the wiro binding of the Maplex brochure, with a metal-ball-link chain in a way that ensures both maximum impact and stand-out quality on architects' shelves.

This entire project was printed in four-color process, but uses environmentally friendly vegetable-based inks. All materials and processes were utilized in a manner that reflects and reinforces the company's contemporary, ethical approach.

ROSS+BUTE

DESIGN
FORM

SPECIFICATIONS
- Two-color lithography
- Matte laminate
- Foil blocking
- Cord handles

Finishing processes play a major role in the design of Ross+Bute's carrier bag and swingtag designs; they have been expertly selected to inform the viewer about the character of the brand and its products. Design company Form used simple two-color litho with matte laminate to create a pleasing waxy finish. On top of this sensual, tactile surface, type is imprinted using silver foil blocking, adding to the luxurious, exclusive, and stylish feel of the design.

EMI MUSIC PUBLISHING "IMAGINE"

DESIGN
AIRSIDE

SPECIFICATIONS
▮ Embossing
▮ Art paper

Airside has created a range of point-of-purchase posters to promote the sales of classic music reissues, including this poster for "Imagine." This design uses only one carefully selected and beautifully executed finishing process: embossing. It is very uncommon to see such large areas of embossing; this process is more usually selected to highlight small areas of focused detail. Here, Airside bravely commissioned an extensive area of embossing in order to subtly highlight and reinforce the meaning of the lyrics.

IMAGINE
ALL THE PEOPLE
LIVING LIFE IN PEACE
YOU MAY SAY THAT I'M A
DREAMER
BUT I'M NOT
THE ONLY ONE
I HOPE SOMEDAY YOU'LL JOIN US
AND THE WORLD
WILL LIVE AS ONE

Airside specified plain, light-colored art paper to highlight the effect of embossing. The edge of each letterform is crisp and appears slightly raised next to the perfectly flat, sunken area created by the die. Overall, this large point-of-purchase poster is an appropriately gentle way of highlighting the meaning of John Lennon's famous lyrics.

CIBO NATURALS

DESIGN
GIORGIO DAVANZO DESIGN

SPECIFICATIONS
▪ Four-color lithography
▪ Adhesive labeling
▪ Silk laminate
▪ Die-cutting

Giorgio Davanzo Design created a range of color-coded labels for Cibo's range of pesto sauces. All five designs utilize four-color lithography to capture the subtleties of the individual variety. The labels can be printed up together, so are cost-effective to produce.

The labels are finished with a layer of silk laminate to give them a stay-clean, wipeable surface that allows each pack to remain bright, clean, and appetizing. They are then die-cut with a circular form that was carefully created to produce stickers that fit within the depression of the lid and allow a consistent and precise amount of the product color and texture to be seen around the edge, reinforcing each variety's link with the color-coding of the label.

The visual character of the circular designs tells any potential purchaser that the product is fresh and of high quality.

The Moving Picture Company
127 Wardour Street, London W1F ONL
Tel: 020 7434 3100. Fax: 020 7287 5187
E-mail: mailbox@moving-picture.com
MPC Online: www.moving-picture.com

The Moving Picture Company

The Moving Picture Company
127 Wardour Street, London W1F ONL
Tel: 020 7434 3100. Fax: 020 7287 5187
E-mail: mailbox@moving-picture.com
MPC Online: www.moving-picture.com

The Moving Picture Company

THE MOVING PICTURE COMPANY

DESIGN
FORM

SPECIFICATIONS
- High-gloss white Chromolux stock
- Single-color printing
- White foil blocking
- Die-cutting

The Moving Picture Company's carrier bags make fascinating use of two finishing processes: foil blocking and die-cutting. Form selected a sturdy, white, high-gloss board and applied bright, single-color blue print across the insides to create a dramatic contrast with the outsides. Company information has been foil-blocked in matte white onto the glossy outer surfaces. This creates a surprising and uncommonly subtle contrast, which implies that The Moving Picture Company produces pleasingly unusual results.

The smaller of these two bags makes interesting use of a cutting form in the creation of its handle, which is punched out in a shape that mimics the Moving Picture Company logo.

TIMBUKTUU COFFEE BAR

DESIGN
SAYLES GRAPHIC DESIGN

SPECIFICATIONS
▌ Two-color lithography
▌ Self-adhesive stock
▌ Die-cutting

These two designs for Timbuktuu coffee bags are unusual because of the striking use of two-color die-cut labels. This might not seem extraordinary in itself, but the labels are quite sizable and noticeable, not only for their bold graphics, but also for their shape: a small label appears to jut out from the side of a larger one. This individual branding has been adhered to off-the-shelf brown bags, creating an economically priced impression of gourmet coffee and exclusivity. (Another example of Sayles' design for Timbuktuu can be seen on page 126).

BAG

SPECTATOR SOLIS

DESIGN
STUDIO INTERNATIONAL

SPECIFICATIONS
▪ Single-color printing
▪ Foil blocking

Studio International used large areas of shiny silver blocking to apply the Spectator Solis logo to this large blue carrier bag. It is very unusual to see such an expanse of foil blocking, but it is one of the most successful ways of producing an area of truly metallic-looking silver.

A secondary result of using foil blocking is the creation of slightly debossed areas; these are produced as a consequence of the block forcing the foil to adhere to the paper stock. In the case of this carrier bag, blocking was done after printing and lamination to ensure that the metallic foil sits firmly on the uppermost surface of the bag, and contrasts with the matte-laminated surface.

CHOCOLAT AU LAIT
AU
THYM

45 g

SUITE 88

DESIGN
PAPRIKA

SPECIFICATIONS
▌ Foil blocking

Paprika uses chocolate-colored foil blocking to imprint branding and typographic details onto labeling for the Canadian boutique chocolatier Suite 88. The blocking process forces a fine layer of colored foil to adhere to the surface of paper or card, and in so doing creates a slight depression, similar to the effect created by debossing.

SUITE 88
CHOCOLATIER

CHOCOLAT BLANC
AUX
AMANDES
45 g

CHOCOLAT NOIR
AU
CHILI CAYENNE
45 g

Suite 88 labeling displays a particularly sophisticated example of foil blocking, as this process has been successfully used to capture the fine detail of small typography. Foil blocking is a fairly costly process, and is used to reinforce the luxurious, bespoke nature of this product.

Paprika designed a number of attractive and clever point-of-purchase displays that involve creating the circular elements of the Suite 88 namestyle in dark chocolate, and simply displaying them centrally on square white platters.

GLOSSARY

Art paper

Uncoated stock

MATERIALS

Art paper
See Coated stock.

Coated stock
A smooth, hard-surfaced paper good for reproducing halftone images. It is created by coating the surface with china clay.

Corrugated board
Highly ridged board, often used for packaging.

Cover paper
Category of thick paper used for products such as posters, menus, folders, and covers of paperback books.

Crack-back label
Self-adhesive labeling with pre-cut backing sheets that break apart (crack apart), making labeling easy to remove.

Deckle-edged paper
Handmade paper with uneven edges that taper off.

DL envelopes
Standard size of UK envelope, designed to take A4 paper (210 x 297mm/8¼ x 11¾in) folded into three.

Duplex paper
Thick paper made by pasting together two thinner sheets that can be of different colors. Also called double-faced paper and two-tone paper.

Polypropylene

Pulp board

Glassine paper
A thin, semitransparent paper often used in photograph albums to protect the images.

Laid paper
Uncoated paper with a pattern of mainly horizontal stripes that form a slight surface texture.

Polypropylene
A flexible plastic sheet available in many different colors, including clear and frosted.

Pressure-sensitive labeling
Labels produced with three layers: paper, transparent adhesive, and backing. When the backing is removed and pressure is applied, the labels adhere to most surfaces.

Pulp board
Uncoated board made from wood pulp.

Stock
Another word for the paper or board used to produce a design.

Uncoated stock
Paper that has a rougher surface than coated paper, and that is both bulkier and more opaque.

Vinyl labeling
Plastic adhesive material, available in many colors.

183

Flexography

Silk-screen printing

Silk-screen printing

PRINTING

Bespoke PANTONE colors
Colors created by mixing inks together to form an individual color that does not appear on PANTONE referencing charts.

CMYK
See Full color.

Digital print
See Laser and Inkjet printing.

Dot gain
This is caused when the dots that make up a halftone image increase in size, due to over-absorbent paper or overinking.

Duotone
Where two colors are printed together to make an image richer and denser in color.

Extender
A substance used to extend and lessen the intensity of PANTONE basic pastel colors.

Flexography
Method of printing on a web press using rubber or plastic plates with raised image and text.

Full color
Almost all mass-produced print uses lithographic inks. As a rule, full-color printing is achieved through the selective combination of four process colors: cyan, magenta, yellow, and black/key (CMYK).

Full-color black
Black created by combining cyan, magenta, and yellow inks.

Halftone
A process used to reproduce an illustration, which involves breaking it up into small dots of different densities to simulate a full tonal range.

Inkjet printing
A type of color printing that uses cyan, magenta, yellow, and black ink that is sprayed through small nozzles onto the page. Available across the entire price spectrum for home use, as well as on commercial machines that create the highest-quality color print attainable.

Laser printing
When images are transferred to paper using laser technology. Toner particles in black or color mark the page and printing takes place directly from artwork without the need for platemaking. This is frequently the most economical form of printing for short runs.

Letterpress printing
A traditional method of printing type, using a series of metal stamps with individual letters cast into the surface. The letters are set into a form, inked up, and pressed onto the paper's surface. The printed sheet becomes more tactile than that produced by conventional offset lithographic printing, because the type becomes debossed into the surface.

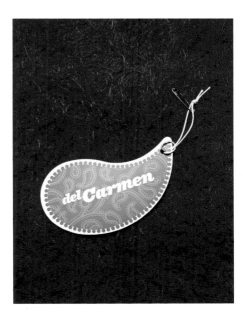

Spot color

Web-fed press

Two passes of ink

Offset lithography
Method of printing using plates with image areas attracting ink and nonimage areas repelling ink. Nonimage areas may be coated with water to repel the oily ink, or may have a surface, such as silicone, that repels ink.

PANTONE Matching System
An international professional color-matching system, which includes colors created out of the four-color set, special individual colors, metallics, fluorescents, and pastels.

PANTONE special
A specific color recipe created by Pantone, Inc. and described by a name or number.

Platemaking
The process of transferring a design from artwork onto a printing plate.

Process colors
See Full color.

Silk-screen printing
A printing method that applies ink onto the surface of the material through a fine silk mesh. This achieves a much denser application of ink than lithography and may be used on an almost limitless variety of surfaces.

Spot color
A special color not generated by the four-color process method.

Spot varnish
See UV varnish.

Tiling
Printing a page layout in sections with overlapping edges so that the pieces can be pasted together.

Tritone
Where three colors are printed together to make an image richer and denser in color.

Two passes of ink
Printing the same color twice, with the second pass of the press printing directly over the first, to create a deeper, more intense result.

Vegetable-based inks
Inks that are made with vegetable-based oils (as opposed to mineral-based, such as petroleum) and that, as a result, are more environmentally friendly.

Web-fed press
Printing press that prints onto a continuous roll of paper. Printing is fast and can be applied to both sides of the paper at once.

Woodblock type
Letters carved in pieces of wood to be relief-printed—similar to letterpress. Traditionally, woodblock type was used for headline and poster work.

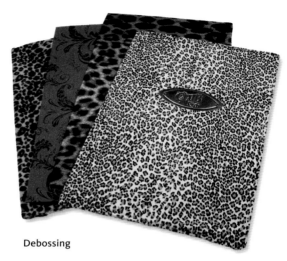
Debossing

Embossing

Holograph

FINISHING

Cutting form
See Die-cut.

Debossed
Having a surface pattern pressed into the page. This process is also known as blind embossing.

Die-cut
A method by which intricate shapes can be cut from a sheet. This requires a custom-made die, which has a sharp steel edge constructed to cut the required shape.

Embossed
Having a raised surface pattern. This is created by using male and female forms.

Foil blocking
See Hot foil stamping.

Heat sealing
A method of welding together two edges of plastic using externally applied heat.

Holograph
Image made with a split laser beam that, when suitably illuminated, shows a three-dimensional image.

Hot foil stamping
Hot foil stamping uses heat and metallic film in a specialty printing process that produces a shiny design on paper, vinyl, textiles, wood, hard plastic, leather, and other materials. Foil stamping is also called hot stamping, dry stamping, foil imprinting, foil blocking, or leaf stamping.

Lamination

Shrink-wrap film

UV varnish

Lamination
The application of a clear matte or gloss protective film over the printed surface of a sheet of paper.

Laser-cutting
A process that produces intricate cutting through most materials using a laser beam.

Machine stitching
Stitching produced using an industrial-strength sewing machine.

Mechanical distressing
Artificial aging imposed by a machine.

Saddle stitching
The standard method of binding. The process involves gathering the pages to be bound and stapling them through the folded edges.

Sealing wax
A durable substance that melts when heated, and can be impressed with a specific mark or monogram to create an individual seal.

Shrink-wrap film
A clear plastic film that is heated so that it shrinks and seals around a product or container to form a tight-fitting layer.

UV varnish
A plastic-based varnish applied by screen printing, available in matte, satin, and gloss finishes. It can be applied over the entire surface or treated as a spot varnish, enabling the designer to print elements in varnish alone or to highlight selected elements on the page.

INDEX

DIRECTORY OF DESIGNERS

Airside
24 Cross Street
London
N1 2BG
UK

Alexander Isley Inc.
9 Brookside Place
Redding
CT 06896
USA

Banker Wessel
Skeppsbron 10
Stockholm
Sweden

Belyea
1809 Seventh Avenue Suite 1250
Seattle
WA 98101
USA

Boing!
47 Roden Avenue
Kidderminster
Worcestershire
DY10 2RE
UK

Bright Pink Communications Design
Lapley Studio
Lapley
Stafford
ST19 9JS
UK

Dotzero Design
208 SW Stark Street 307
Portland
OR 97204
USA

Elfen
20 Harrowby Lane
Cardiff Bay
CF10 5GN
UK

Form
47 Tabernacle Street
London
EC2A 4AA
UK

Gee + Chung Design
38 Bryant Street Suite 100
San Francisco
CA 94105
USA

Giorgio Davanzo Design
232 Belmont Avenue East #506
Seattle
WA 98102
USA

Ideas Frescas
Edificio Eben Ezer Blvd Sur
San Salvador
El Salvador

IE Design + Communications
422 Pacific Coast Highway
Hermosa Beach
CA 90254
USA

Inksurge
171 Cordillera Street
Sta Mesa Heights
Quezon City
1100
Philippines

KBDA
2558 Overland Avenue
Los Angeles
CA 90064
USA

Kendall Ross Brand Development and Design
1904 Third Avenue Suite 1005
Seattle
WA 98101
USA

KROG, Ljubljana
Krakovski nasip 22 1000
Ljubljana
Slovenia

Laura Varsky
Av Rivadavia 14
405 Villa Sarmiento
Buenos Aires
CP 1706
Argentina

Louise Carrier Graphic Design
26 Elliotts Lane
Codsall
Wolverhampton
WV8 1PG
UK

Matt Graif Design
509 W. Olive
Springfield
MD 65806
USA

Montezuma's Chocolates Ltd.
Birdham Business Park
Chichester
PO20 7BT
UK

MSLK
22–23 33rd Road
Long Island City
NY 11106
USA

Palazzolo Design
6410 Knapp NE
Ada
MI 49301
USA

Paprika
400 Laurier W #610
Montreal QC
H21 2K7
Canada

Pear Design Inc.
1440 North Drayton #204
Chicago
IL 60622
USA

Plain Lazy Ltd.
Unit 1
The Cliffe Industrial Estate
Lewes
East Sussex
UK

Plazm Media Inc.
PO Box 2863
Portland
OR 97208
USA

Prank Design
71 Summer Street 6th Floor
Boston
MA 02110
USA

R2 Design
Rua de Meinedo no 112-4100-337
Porto
Portugal

Rinzen
Brunnenstrasse 10 2 HH 1.0G
Berlin
10119
Germany

Ruckley
Stanton Farm
Ruckley Estate
Shifnal
Shropshire
TF11 8PQ
UK

Sagmeister, Inc.
222 West 14 Street
New York City
NY 10011
USA

Sayles Graphic Design
3701 Beaver Avenue
Des Moines
IA 50310
USA

Sheaff Dorman Purins
186 Crescent Road
Needham
MA 02494
USA

Shimokochi-Reeves
832 Cole Avenue
Los Angeles
CA 90038-2609
USA

Sonsoles Llorens Disseny Grafic
Casp 56 Esc. D 4rt
Barcelona
08010
Spain

Source Inc.
116 South Michigan Avenue
Chicago
IL 60603
USA

Steven Wilson
67 Richmond Street
Brighton
BN2 9PE
UK

Stormhouse Partners
425 West 23rd Street #1F
New York City
NY 10011
USA

Studio International
Buconjiceva 43
Zagreb
10000
Croatia

Studio Output
2 Broadway
Lace Market
Nottingham
NG1 1PS
UK

Subplot Design Inc.
The Mercantile Building
318 Homer Street, Suite 301
Vancouver BC
V6B 2V2
Canada

The Bath House Ltd.
The Grain Store
Bosk Lane
Sedbergh
LA10 5HF
UK

The Small Stakes
1847 5th Avenue
Oakland
CA 94606
USA

Train Of Thought
3834 92nd Street
Seattle
Washington
98115
USA

V4 Studio
Cadbury Trebor Bassett
Bournville
Birmingham
B30 2LU
UK

Vault49
10 East 23rd Street Suite 300
New York City
NY 10010
USA

Vrontikis Design Office
2707 Westwood Blvd
Los Angeles
CA 90064
USA

White Stuff
Tuborg House
Mandrell Road
London
SW2 5DL
UK

Wunderburg Design
Innere Laufer Gasse 11
Nuremberg
90403
Germany

Zion Graphics
Bellmansgatan
Stockholm
11820
Sweden

ABOUT THE AUTHORS

Jessica Glaser and Carolyn Knight are partners in the UK design firm Bright Pink, which serves clients in industries including textiles, health care, finance and nonprofit organizations. Both are senior lecturers in Graphic Communications within the University of Wolverhampton School of Art and Design. Their previous books include: *Create Impact with Type, Image & Color*, and *Sticky Graphics*, both published by RotoVision.

ACKNOWLEDGMENTS

We would like to extend our thanks to everyone who has helped in the creation of this book, including The University of Wolverhampton, RotoVision, and all the designers who so kindly submitted work.